# SIGRID HOLMWO

## 1857 - Paintings

16 January - 23 February 2008

## Annely Juda Fine Art

23 Dering Street (off New Bond Street)
London W1S 1AW
ajfa@annelyjudafineart.co.uk
www.annelyjudafineart.co.uk
Tel   020 7629 7578   Fax   020 7491 2139
Monday - Friday 10 - 6   Saturday 11 - 5

Cover: **Church Boats** 2007  fluorescent egg tempera; lead white, iron oxide, raw Siena, Spanish glazing ochre, red lead, French ultramarine in oils; birch leaf lake in pine resin on board  137 x 122 cm

## You don't need to follow the rules all the time

The film critic David Thomson has written of Jacques Demy that of all the New Wave directors who once professed their joy in cinema, he remained most faithful to the delights of sight and sound and to the romance of movie iconography. With loving attention to those towns that line the Atlantic coast where he grew up and which he immortalised in films like *Les Parapluies de Cherbourg* and *Les Demoiselles de Rochefort*, Demy invented a world of benign and enchanting imagination, 'as distinguished and ennobling as, say, *Les Très Riches Heures du Duc de Berry*'. He was, says Thomson, a poetic realist.

Sigrid Holmwood is also a poetic realist who believes that fantasy is a part of the reality of life. Reconstructing the work of a painter of peasant life, she uses hand-made historical paints applied with period brushes. The specific pigments, binding media and handling properties emphasise colour and luminosity and evoke comparisons with sixteenth-century landscape and genre painting and nineteenth-century Impressionism. Her paintings generate powerful emotions, and display an exuberance combined with a sublime sense of absurdity, shot through with an almost constant sense of nostalgia. As with Demy's films, the coexistence of this strangeness and intensity might make some viewers recoil in disbelief and regard the whole spectacle as an esoteric piece of camp. Even so, nobody can doubt the artist's sincerity.

Holmwood studied at the Ruskin School of Drawing and Fine Art in the late 1990s. Initially, her paintings were based on still photographs derived from her own video footage. These paintings bore a superficial resemblance to the voluptuous representational canvases that Richard Diebenkorn was producing in the 1950s and 1960s, but Holmwood was just as interested in the work of Gillian Carnegie, Peter Doig and Luc Tuymans, artists who were 'getting away with figurative painting' when figurative painting was regarded with not a little scepticism.

The Ruskin is one of very few British art schools that oblige their students to study art history, and it was while she was in Oxford that Holmwood started to pay attention to the work of the Old Masters. 'You can look at old paintings', says Holmwood, 'and steal things from them and that's okay, you're seen as cultured, but if you look at contemporary paintings and steal things from them then that's regarded as derivative. It always felt easier to grab things from the past.' Holmwood was aware that it was not done to declare an allegiance to Pieter Bruegel the Elder or Claude Monet in the last years of the twentieth century. There was an unspoken compulsion to keep looking to present-day sources. Yet despite her respect for contemporary painters, Holmwood resisted being directly influenced by them. 'You're always looking to carve out your own place,' she explains, 'and articulate your own voice, to be different from your peers.'

In her pursuit of difference, the artist turned to the world of cinema for inspiration. As an undergraduate, Holmwood was especially keen on the films of Dogme95, the avant-garde film making movement begun by the Danish directors Lars von Trier and Thomas Vinterberg. The Dogme collective aimed to purify film making by refusing special effects and postproduction modifications. The emphasis on purity forced von Trier, Vinterberg and others to focus on the actual story and on the actors' performances, and Holmwood endeavoured to translate this clarifying ethos into her painting.

The artist embarked on a postgraduate degree in painting at the Royal College of Art in 2000. Here, she found herself mark making for its own sake and Diana Thater came to succeed Carnegie, Doig and Tuymans in her artistic affections. Referencing Thater's large-scale, multiprojection video installations, which focused on the intersection between nature and culture, Holmwood's canvases began to manifest an all-over quality in which the subject could only be discerned from a distance. By the time of her final show in 2002, Holmwood was transmitting a genuine concern for the complexity of painting and its ability to chart multi-dimensional space, and her video-derived depictions of figures had been replaced by abstract depictions of grass and dense undergrowth.

In her second year at the Royal College, Holmwood produced a large watercolour of a figure in a landscape. It was when she returned to painting in oil and acrylic that she began to take a real interest in the creative possibilities offered up by glazing. Until then, Holmwood had worked mostly *alla prima*. Glazing provided her with a more nuanced way of laying down paint and greatly expanded her pictorial and expressive repertoire. Around this time, she was also given a copy of *Bright Earth: Art and the Invention of Color* in which the popular science writer Philip Ball examines some of the tools and materials that chemists have added to the painter's palette, and the physical and cultural factors that condition our perceptions of colour.

*Bright Earth* was a revelation for Holmwood. It made her think closely about colour, and especially how she might make use of brightly coloured grounds in her work. Just as importantly, it sparked an interest in the technical aspects of paint production and how artists manufactured and employed paint in the sixteenth and nineteenth centuries. 'I started to think about how I could incorporate all this knowledge about how paint was used in the Renaissance,' she explains, 'while retaining something of the spontaneous feel of Impressionist painting. I wanted to use planning and foresight to make my work glow. I always want my paintings to look wet and shiny. I never want them to appear chalky and dry. When I look at a painting, I imagine it being made, and I want a certain juiciness to be apparent in my work.'

Holmwood stopped using video footage as a point of departure for her paintings after she received an invitation to apply for the Sainsbury Scholarship in Painting and Sculpture at the British School in Rome. The Sainsbury Scholarship is open to artists who can demonstrate a commitment to drawing in their practice. With the stimulus of the invitation, Holmwood decided to give herself over to drawing from life for the first time in her career: 'Because my work relates to Impressionism, I had almost talked my way out of drawing theoretically. I'd got involved in the whole *disegni* versus *colori* debate. Now I've always preferred the Venetians and there's always been this idea that the Impressionists didn't draw, but the Venetians did draw and so did the Impressionists. Why wasn't I drawing?'

Formerly Holmwood had subsumed her interest in line and space in her pre-paratory work with video. In order to put together a portfolio to accompany what turned out to be her successful application for the Sainsbury Scholarship, she produced works on paper with coloured pencils. This enabled her to draw with colour, and she translated her earliest drawing of a tree into a painting. 'I found myself thinking this is just so much better, so much freer,' she confesses. 'Under the influence of Dogme95, I had created all these boundaries for myself. Maybe that's a good thing to do for a while, when you're finding your feet, but ultimately that wasn't the point. That was only a means to getting somewhere new. You don't need to follow the rules all the time.'

The selection of four paintings from her *Woodland Series* for New Contemporaries in 2003 represented something of a watershed for the artist for the exhibition included three pieces derived from video footage and the painting from her first drawing. At the same time as she was exploring her nascent interest in working from life, Holmwood's focus moved from the human figure to landscape. In Rome the artist was making drawings of trees in the Borghese Gardens: 'I recognised the trees from Renaissance paintings and from the canvases of Claude and Poussin. The trees that previously belonged only to art history were suddenly there in front of me and I was able to see how they fitted in.' Going to Italy gave Holmwood

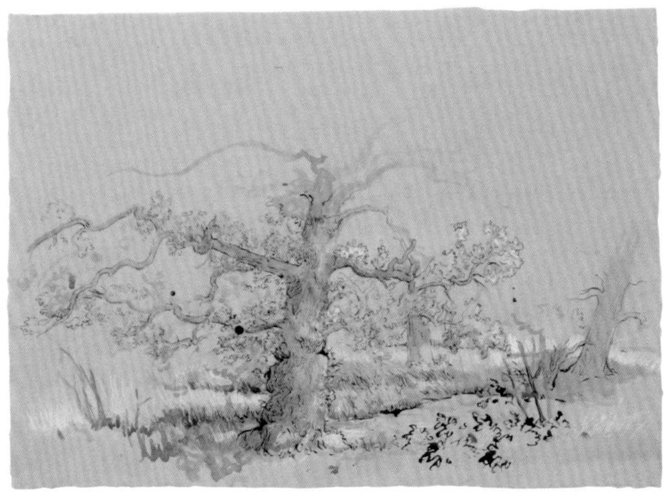

**Study for 'Woodland Pasture with Oaks'**   2007
pen, ink and gouache on paper
37 x 50.5 cm

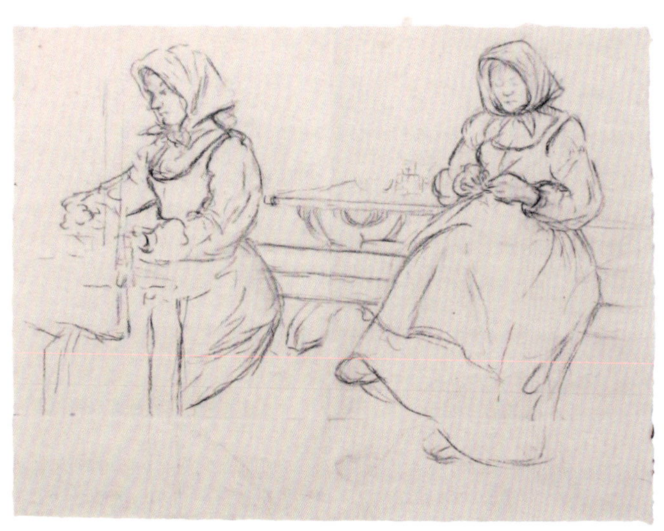

1  **The Spinners**  2007
fluorescent yellow orange egg tempera; lead white, Chrome yellow
light, Prussian blue, Cochineal, bone black, Spanish glazing ochre
in oils on board
122 x 153 cm

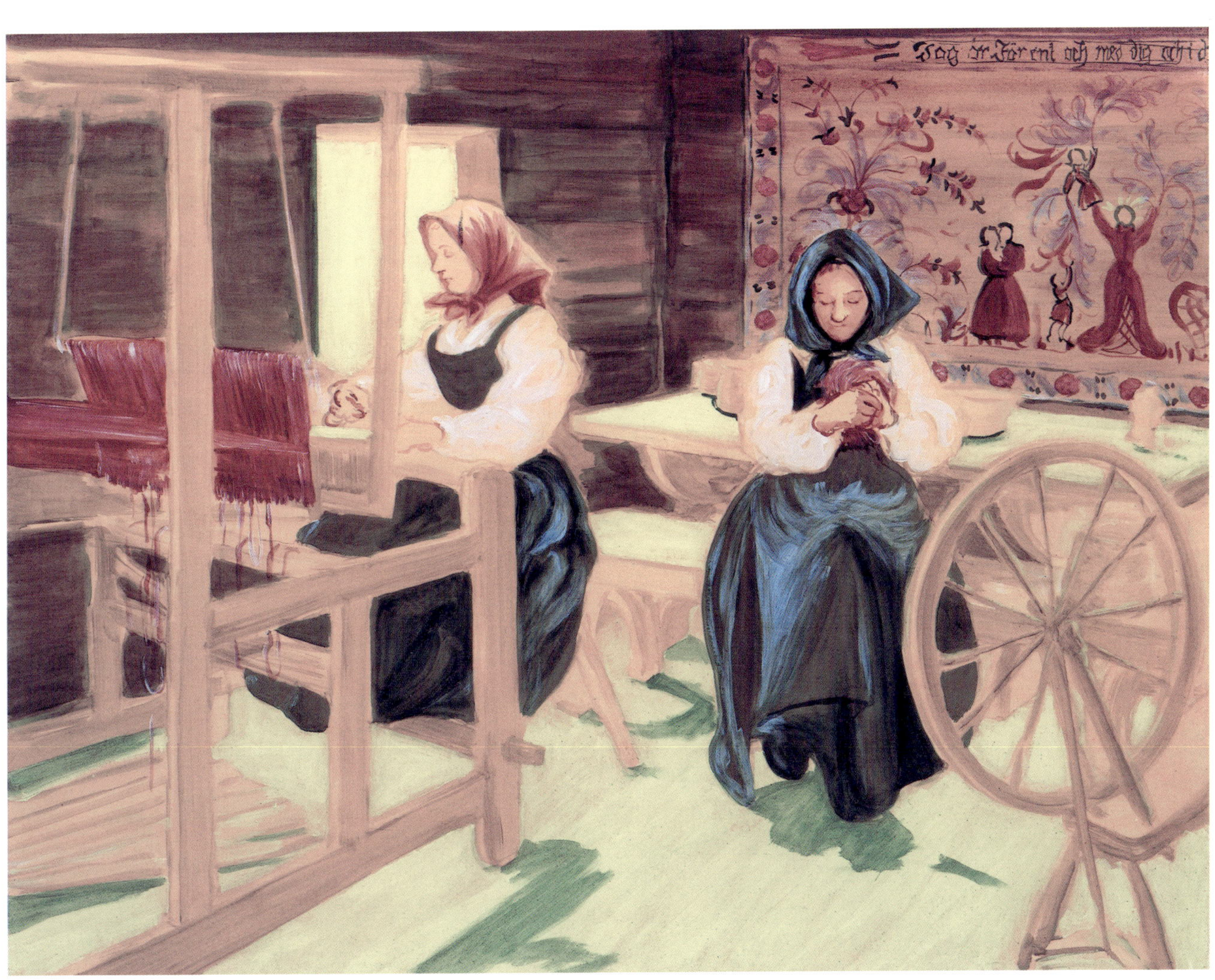
Jag är Förent och med dig wid d

permission to look at these artists more seriously and to make work that referenced sixteenth- and seventeenth-century landscape painting. Mimicking the artist on the Grand Tour, she realised that she had assumed the mantle of a historical re-enactor.

'It seemed to me to be important that I was drawing from life, as those earlier artists did,' explains Holmwood. 'In drawing from life you are having an encounter with something real. In contemporary art there is such an obsession with things not being real, with everything being a cultural construction, a simulacrum. Ultimately, I think I've always been in search of the real. One of the reasons I'm interested in drawing trees is because you've got all these leaves and you need to come up with a solution to a very obvious problem which is how are you going to render all these leaves? There are art historical precedents for that so you can call on art historical solutions to solve a contemporary artistic problem.'

Holmwood's drawings from this period give off the aura of accuracy, but there are moments of invention, just as there are in the work of the Old Masters: 'You have this encounter with something real, but then your imagination starts to kick in and as you're drawing you begin to imagine another place – the place of the drawing. The evolution that takes place on paper is vitally important, especially when the drawing gets converted into a painting.' Rather than fending off reality with the distancing medium of video, Holmwood was now embracing it in order to create a parallel reality, firstly with the drawings and subsequently with the paintings.

After the Sainsbury Scholarship it was but a small step for the artist to get more actively involved in the whole re-enactment industry. Searching the internet for re-enactors, Holmwood came across Louisa Gidney, an archaeologist who hires herself out as a peasant in different historical periods. Gidney trades under the name Rent A Peasant and provides an insight into every-day aspects of rural life in the past. While the military and nobility feature large in historical re-enactment, Rent A Peasant offers up a picture of the basic food-

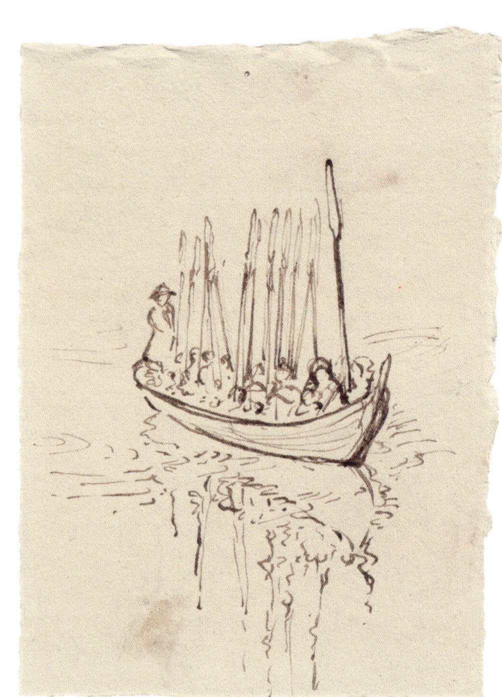

**Study for 'Church Boats'** 2007
ink on paper
17 x 12.5 cm

producing farmer. Holmwood realised that she was drawn to the peasantry for political reasons and hired Gidney so that she could paint her in period costume.

It was Gidney who encouraged Holmwood to immerse herself fully in the re-enactment scene. Holmwood was already grinding her own colours in Rome, using genuine pigments that she had read about in science books and restoration reports. When she returned to London, she took a job as a warder at the National Gallery as a means of spending time with the works of the lesser-known Old Masters, and even considered reapplying to the Royal College to undertake an interdisciplinary doctorate in painting and conservation as a means of learning more about paint reconstruction. 'Analysing binders is very difficult,' says Holmwood. 'We know that there are proteins in there, but do these proteins come from egg, milk or animal skin?' I wanted to know these things, but then it struck me that it would be far more interesting to do this research myself and that was when I got properly involved with the re-enactors.'

During the course of her research, Holmwood alighted on the site for the Original Re-enactors Market. The Market is the largest European forum for manufacturers and traders producing goods for re-enactors and historical interpreters and features stalls of people from different periods selling items that are simulta-neously authentic and counterfeit. 'On the one hand there is all this fantasy in play,' says Holmwood, 'and on the other there is this genuine market where people are trading their wares. This got me thinking even more about what constitutes reality and authenticity. Of course there's a strange play element in re-enacting a period of history, but there's also something deeply authentic about it, about being in control of your materials and processes. Everything becomes connected.'

Holmwood visited the Original Re-enactors Market outside Coventry and elected to become a member of the Tudor Group. The Tudor Group describes itself as an historical interpretation society and has a reputation for historical accuracy. Their clothing, for example, is hand-stitched and the construction techniques are drawn from surviving examples and other primary sources. When she is with the Group, Holmwood is researching sixteenth-century painting techniques and adopts the persona of a peasant-painter. The work that emerged from spending a week with the Group at the Weald and Downland Open-Air Museum was shown at Frieze Art Fair in 2006 and in the solo exhibition *Past-times and Re-creation* at the Transition Gallery.

The paintings and drawings in *1857 - Paintings* follow on from the Tudor Group project and its peasant focus stems from her recent travels in Sweden. In 2006, the artist visited the open-air museum Skansen and the province of Dalarna as well as her mother's family's farm in Västergötland. Skansen is the oldest open-air museum in the world and contains a unique collection of historical buildings. The Swedes are passionate about their past and farming communities retain their customs and ways of life. The buildings at Skansen have been sourced from rural locations across Sweden, including Dalarna, and people work on site in original costume. Dalarna has a well-defined craft tradition in which painting features prominently. The province was home to the noted nineteenth-century artists Anders Zorn and Carl Larsson, who were both painters of peasant life, and has come to symbolise the very essence of Swedishness.

A number of the pieces in the current exhibition represent scenes from the annual midsummer celebrations in Dalarna, including traditional dances and the arrival of the church boat. Others portray interiors and exteriors and rites of passage, such as betrothals and weddings. The artist uses authentic, eighteenth- and nineteenth-century pigments, like Prussian blue, Chrome yellow and Viridian green for her glazes. She has also prepared a pigment from birch leaves that the peasant-painters used to depict leaves - 'an interesting conflation of material and meaning' - and she makes use of sour milk as a binder, which allows for the production of trompe-l'oeil mahogany patterning. The peasant-painters used this technique to vary the otherwise uniform surfaces of their pinewood buildings and furniture.

Holmwood takes pleasure in generating a wide range of colours from the fewest possible pigments. Notwithstanding their almost hallucinatory qualities, many of the colours have a basis in reality. The artist describes them as 'heightened', and while her paintings make no pretence at naturalism Holmwood will reject colours if they appear too extreme. 'I don't want to be seen to be piling on colours just for the sake of it,' she argues. 'They have to make sense in the world of the painting.' There is a logic and reality to that world. It might not be our world, but neither are the worlds described by Glenn Brown, John Currin and Elizabeth Peyton, yet all convey an internal integrity that obliges us to consider them on their own terms.

Most of the works in *1857 - Paintings* depict actual scenes although some of the imagery, like the linen harvest and the portrait of the last Dalarna peasant-painter and his wife peeling potatoes, derive from photographs in the Leksands Konst-museum. Holmwood is obsessed with function and use value and these interests surface time and again in scenes of harvesting, milling, spinning and weaving. For Holmwood painting and weaving are related actions, characterised by interlacing and varying degrees of transparency. This connection is succinctly visualised in *The Spinners* (cat. no. 1), a painting that urges comparison with Velázquez's canvas of the same name, for both show women at work and both are representations that contain depictions of other representations.

'Of particular interest to me is Svetlana Alpers' interpretation of *The Spinners*,' Holmwood says, 'as Velázquez finding a way to meditate on his relationship to art history and his contemporaries without direct copying. Rubens did a copy of Titian's *Rape of Europa* on a visit to the court in Spain, which Velázquez would have seen. Velázquez turned the same painting into a tapestry as a comment on creative competition. In the background of my painting, I have depicted a version of Adam Heinrich Müller's *Celestial Kiss of Love*. It is a favourite motif of the peasant-painter Mats Anders Olsson and was taken from Müller's pietistic devotional manual, which records God kissing someone and this heavenly love being passed on through the family tree. This moment holds up a mirror to the unfaithful Zeus in the *Rape of Europa*. The Swedish text in the painting reads: 'I am with you and one with you and with your family always'. My use of Velázquez and Olsson posits a relationship to art history and artists that emphasises something being given and passed on as a statement on the supremacy of cultural inheritance over competition.'

Holmwood's fascination with paintings that include other artworks resonates with her interest in the trompe-l'oeil techniques that the peasant-painters used on their buildings and furniture. In each instance, painting is operating at the interface between the literal and the representational, between the real and the unreal. 'I'm not one of these artists who believes in emptying things out,' states Holmwood. 'I went there in the past and got bored. What I like is the way meanings are created in harmony with the materials. There is a path through painting in contemporary art whereby serious painters are seen to do the abstract stuff and then there are the less serious artists who are into narrative, where the technique is less relevant. I don't see why you can't do both. The process of making the work and things that I do, like joining the Tudor Group and going to the open-air museums and drawing from life, are all relevant. It's part of what my work is about, but there's also a make-believe world being created from those interests.'

Holmwood's paintings and drawings show us the nature of art as a thoughtful and sometimes melodramatic medium. To adapt David Thomson's comments on Jacques Demy's movies, they signal a way ahead, and a means to dispel the fatuous notion that because painting has the capacity to render lifelike scenes it has to be life itself. Painting may be dead, but in Holmwood's hands the poetic potential of realist painting continues to thrive.

Paul Bonaventura, Senior Research Fellow in Fine Art
Studies, University of Oxford, January 2008

2   **The Linen Harvest**  2007
Prussian blue, Cadmium yellow, zinc white, fluorescent red in
egg tempera; lead white, Chrome yellow deep, Prussian blue,
lead antimonate, iron oxide in oils on board
122 x 153 cm

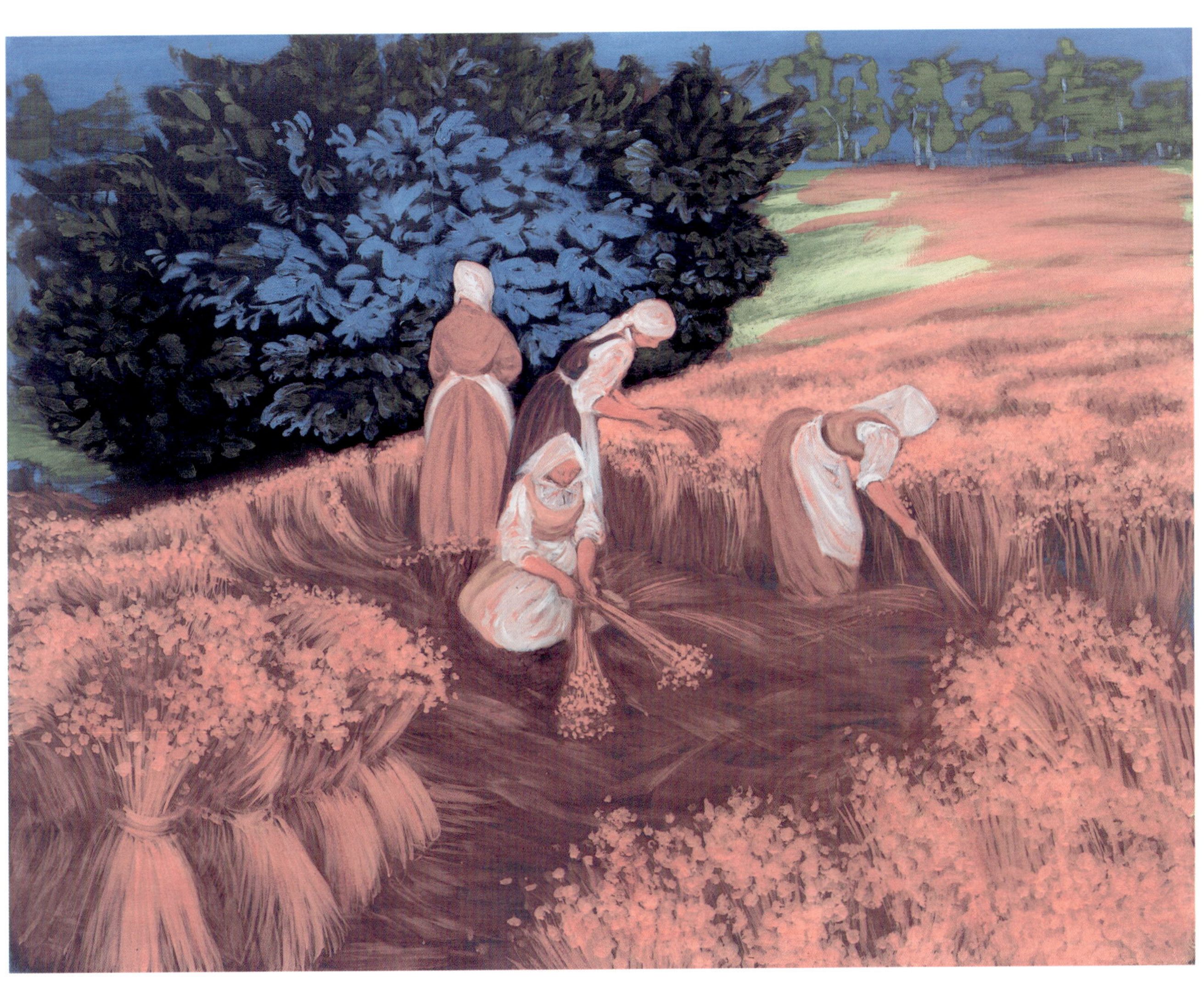

3   **Birch Bark Shoes**  2007
fluorescent yellow orange, Prussian blue, zinc white in egg
tempera; raw Siena, lead white, French ultramarine,
Chrome yellow light in oils on board
102 x 122 cm

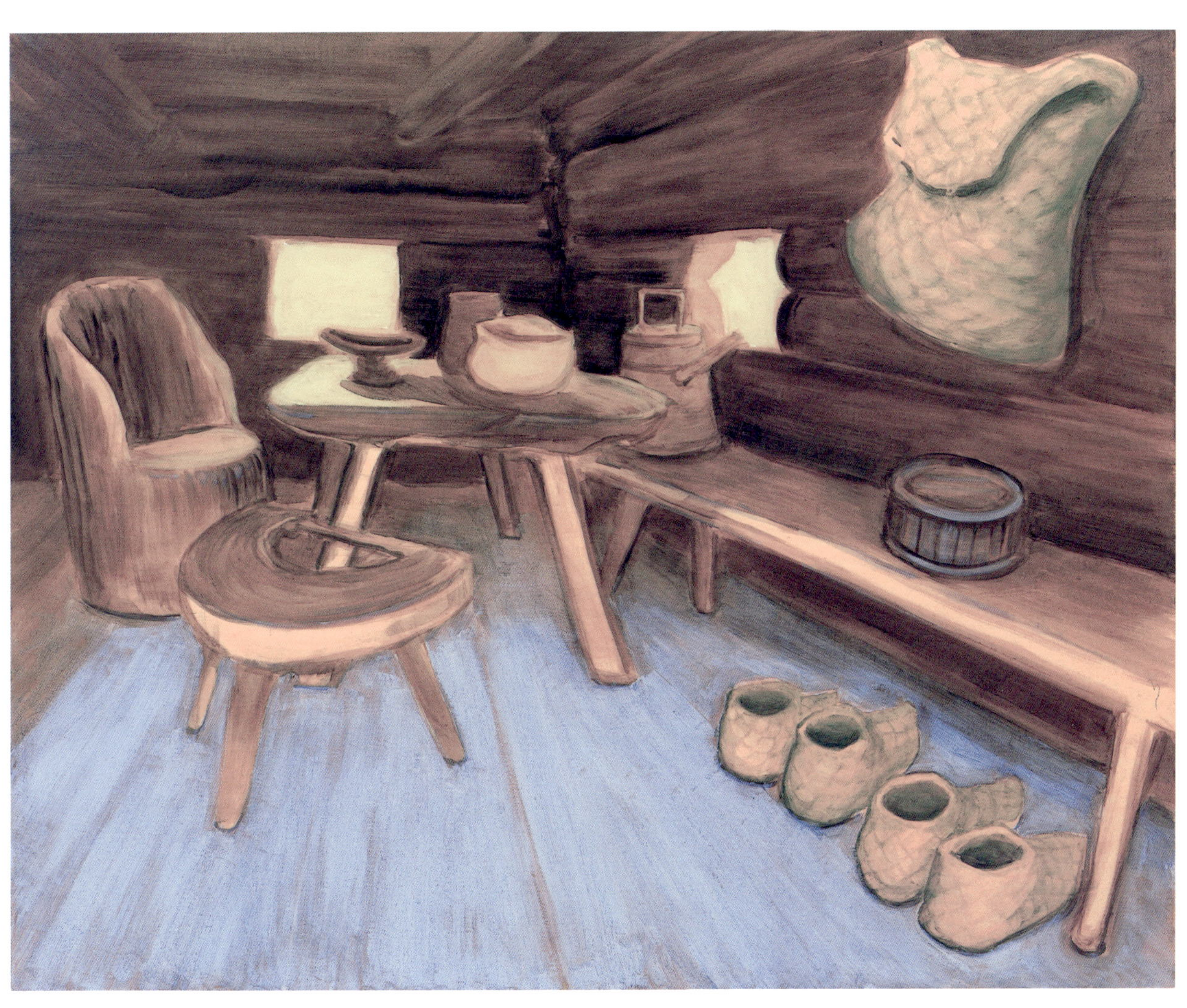

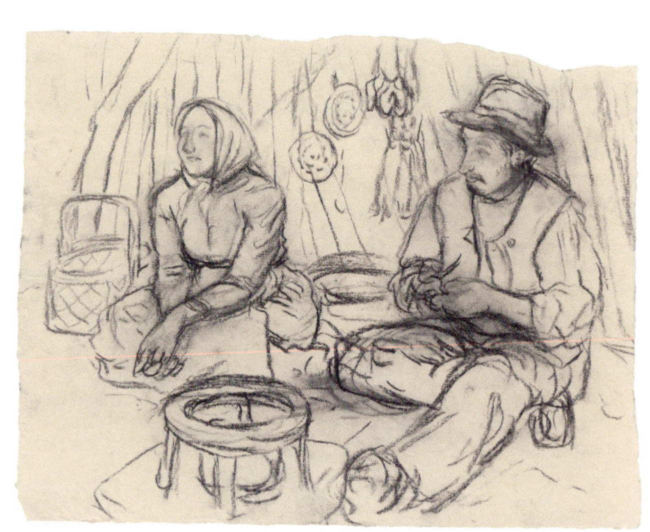

4  **Sámi Couple**  2007
fluorescent yellow orange, fluorescent flame red egg tempera;
Chrome yellow, lead white, Cochineal, madder, French ultramarine,
Prussian blue, lead antimonate, Viridian in oils on board
61 x 75 cm

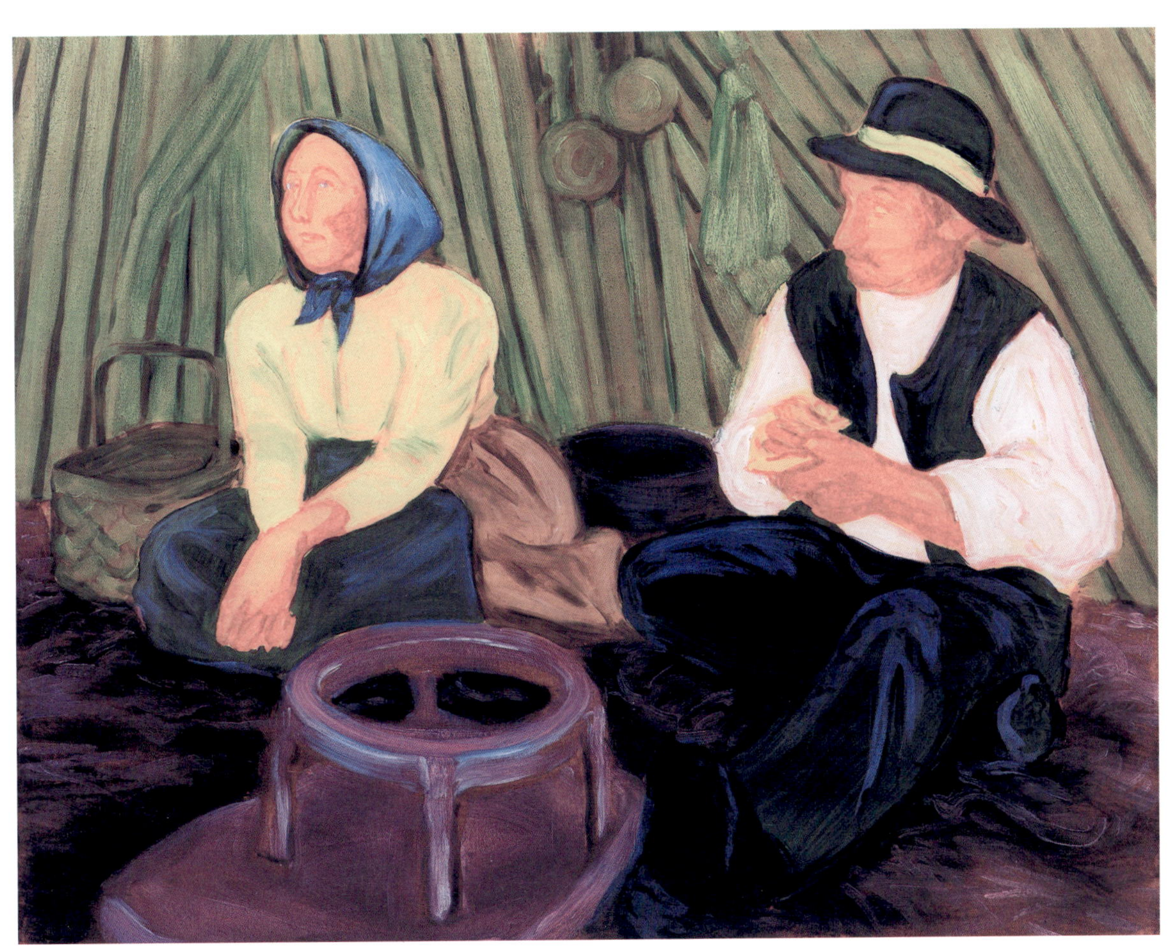

5    **Church Boats**  2007
fluorescent egg tempera; lead white, iron oxide, raw Siena, Spanish
glazing ochre, red lead, French ultramarine in oils; birch leaf lake in
pine resin on board
137 x 122 cm

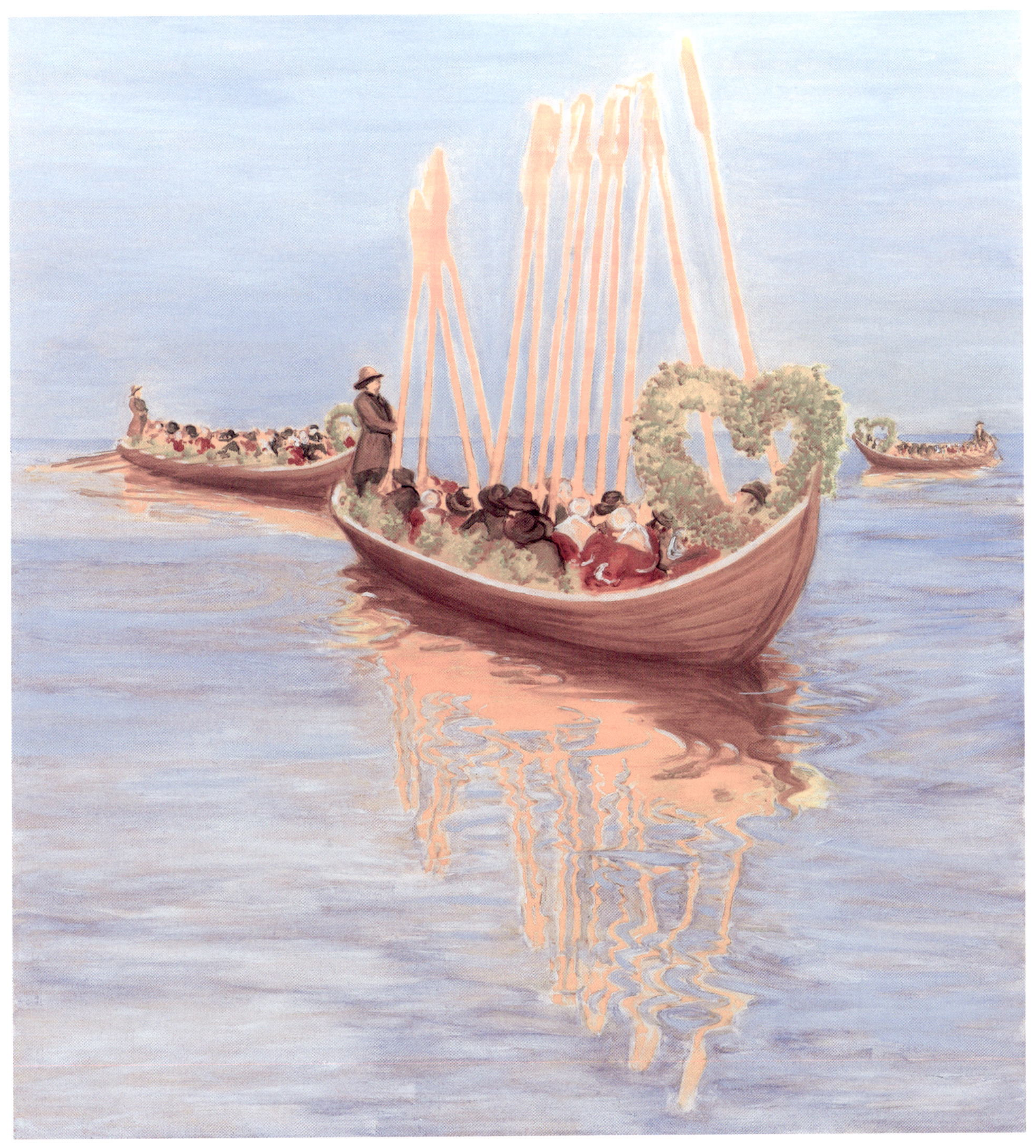

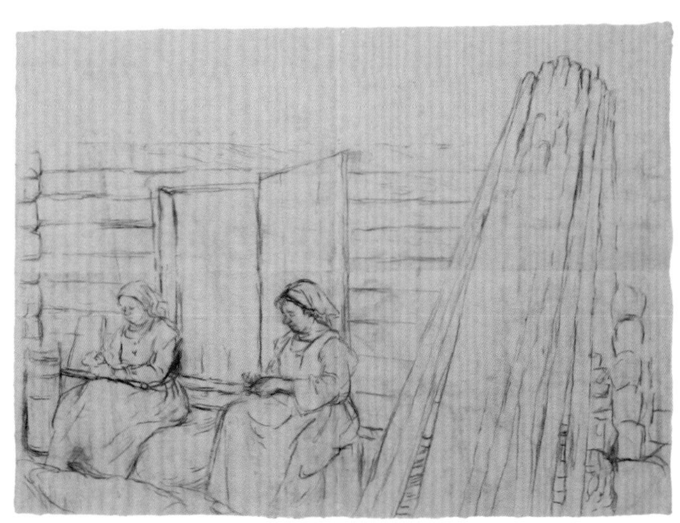

6    **Finn Settlement**  2007
fluorescent yellow orange egg tempera; Cochineal, madder,
lead white, Cobalt turquoise, French ultramarine, Viridian,
Chrome green in oils on board
61 x 75 cm

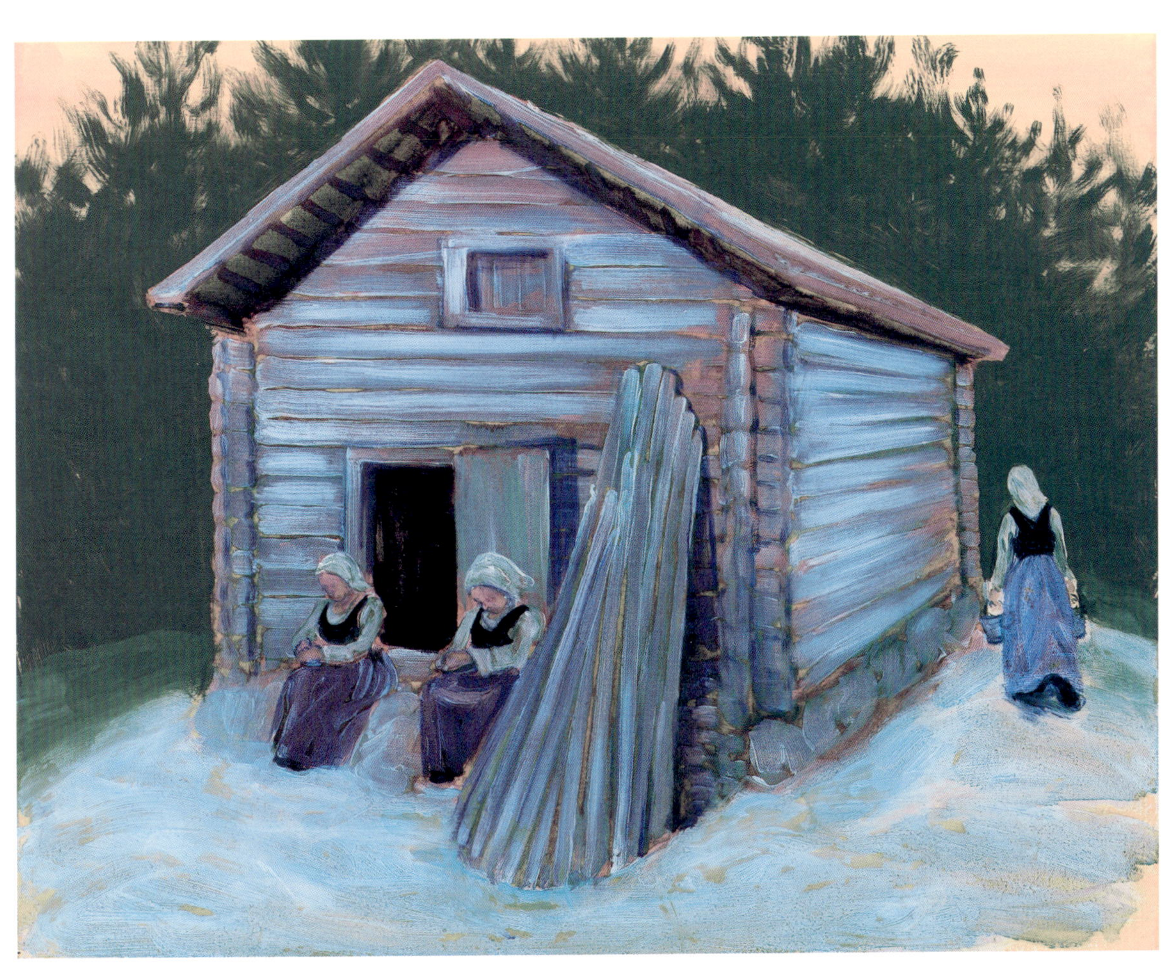

7    **Midsummer Pole**  2007
Cadmium lemon yellow, fluorescent lemon yellow, fluorescent yellow orange,
fluorescent red egg tempera; Chrome yellow, Viridian, red lead, lead
white, Prussian blue, iron oxide in oils; birch leaf lake in pine resin on board
107 x 122 cm

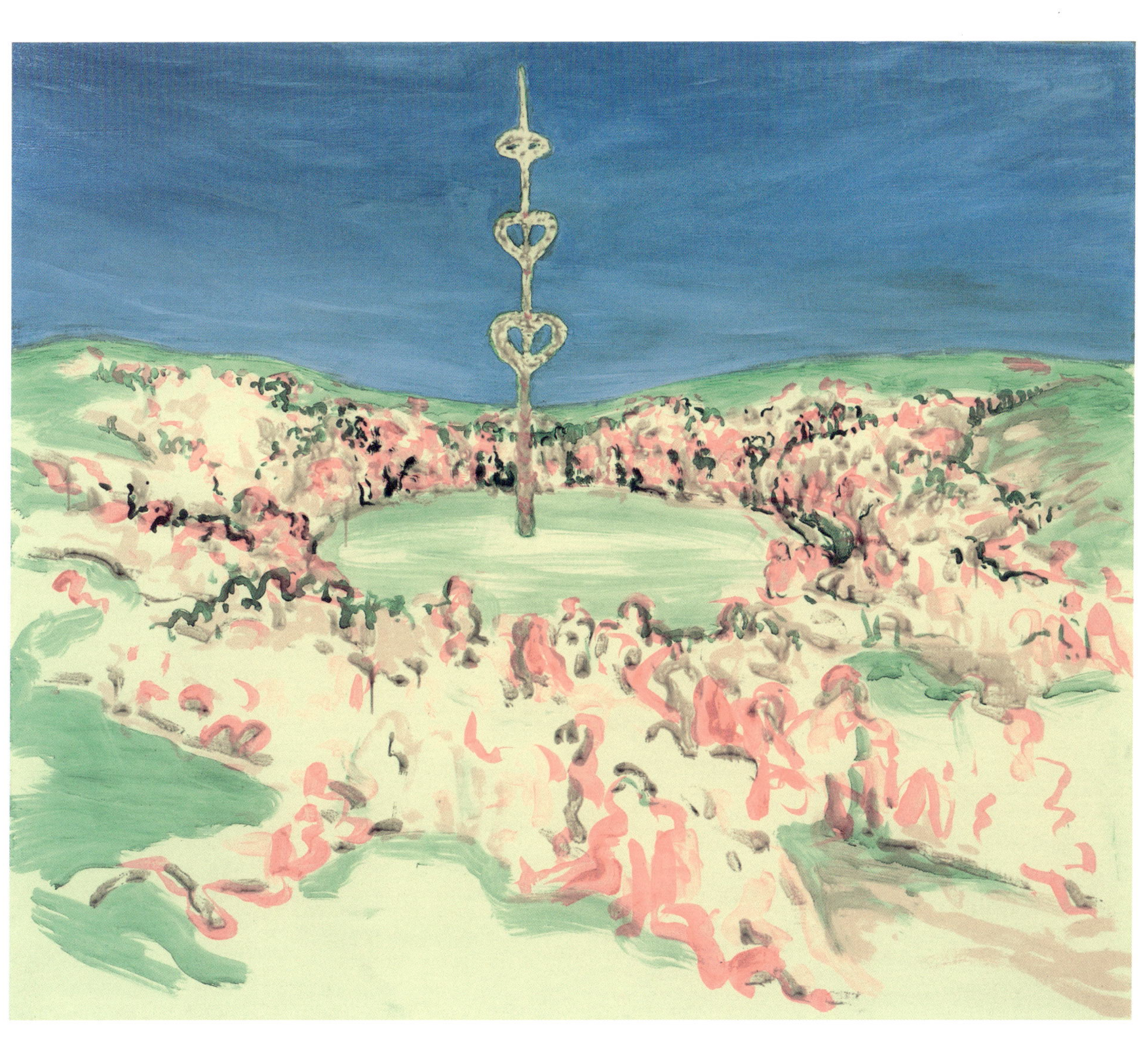

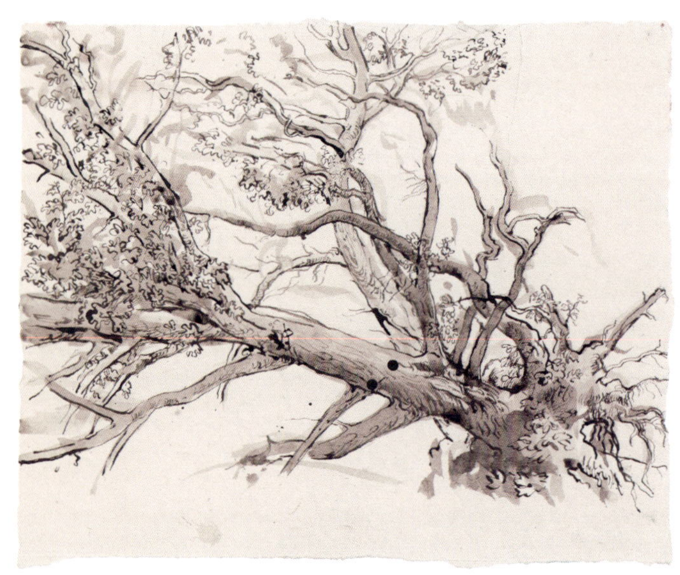

8    **Fallen Oaks**  2007
Cobalt turquoise egg tempera; Prussian blue, French gold ochre,
Viridian, Bohemian green earth, lead white in oils; fluorescent
yellow orange in soured milk on board
137 x 122 cm

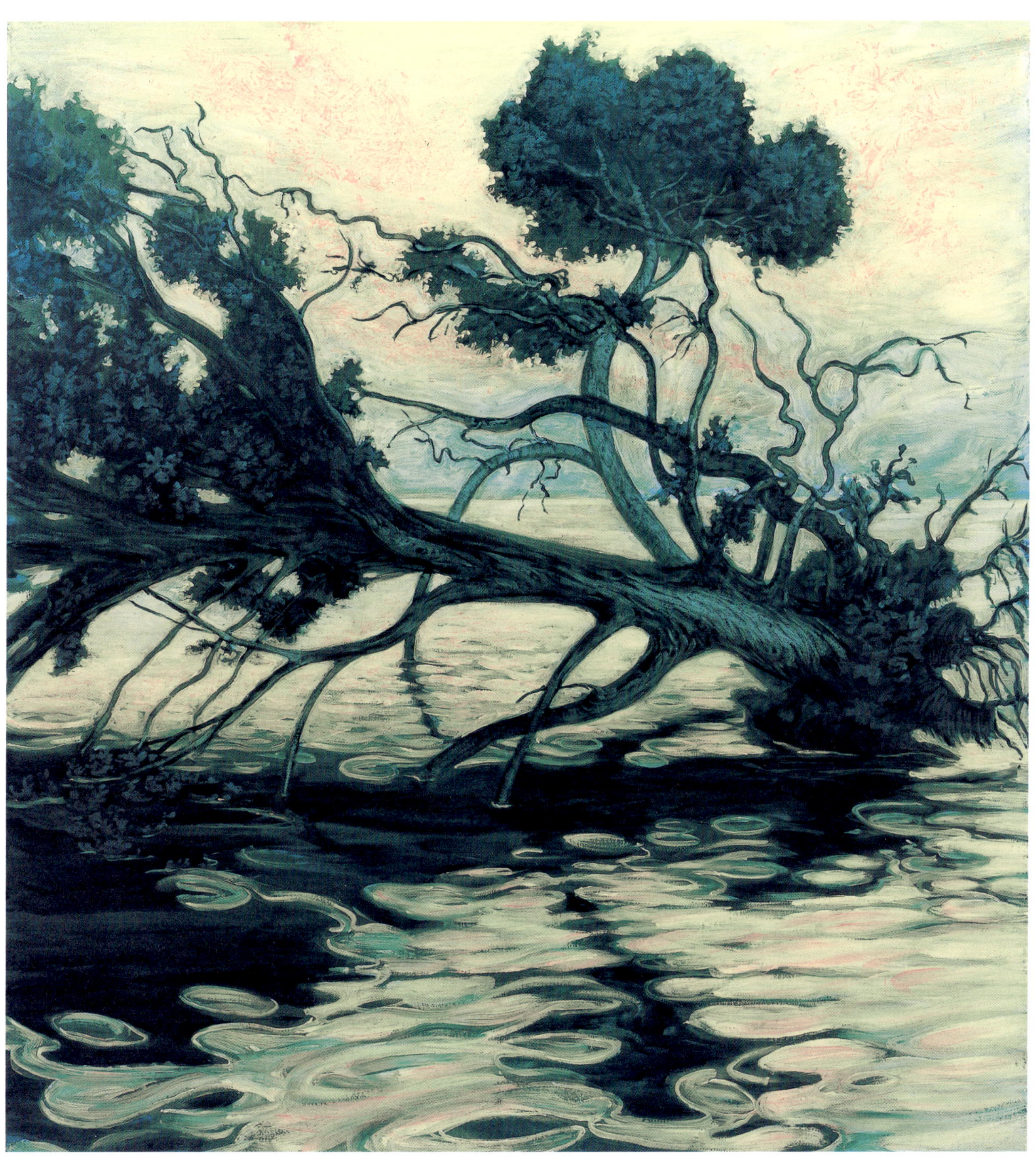

9   **Woodland Pasture with Oaks**  2007
fluorescent orange egg tempera; Chrome yellow,
lead white, Chrome green, Viridian in oils on board
91 x 122 cm

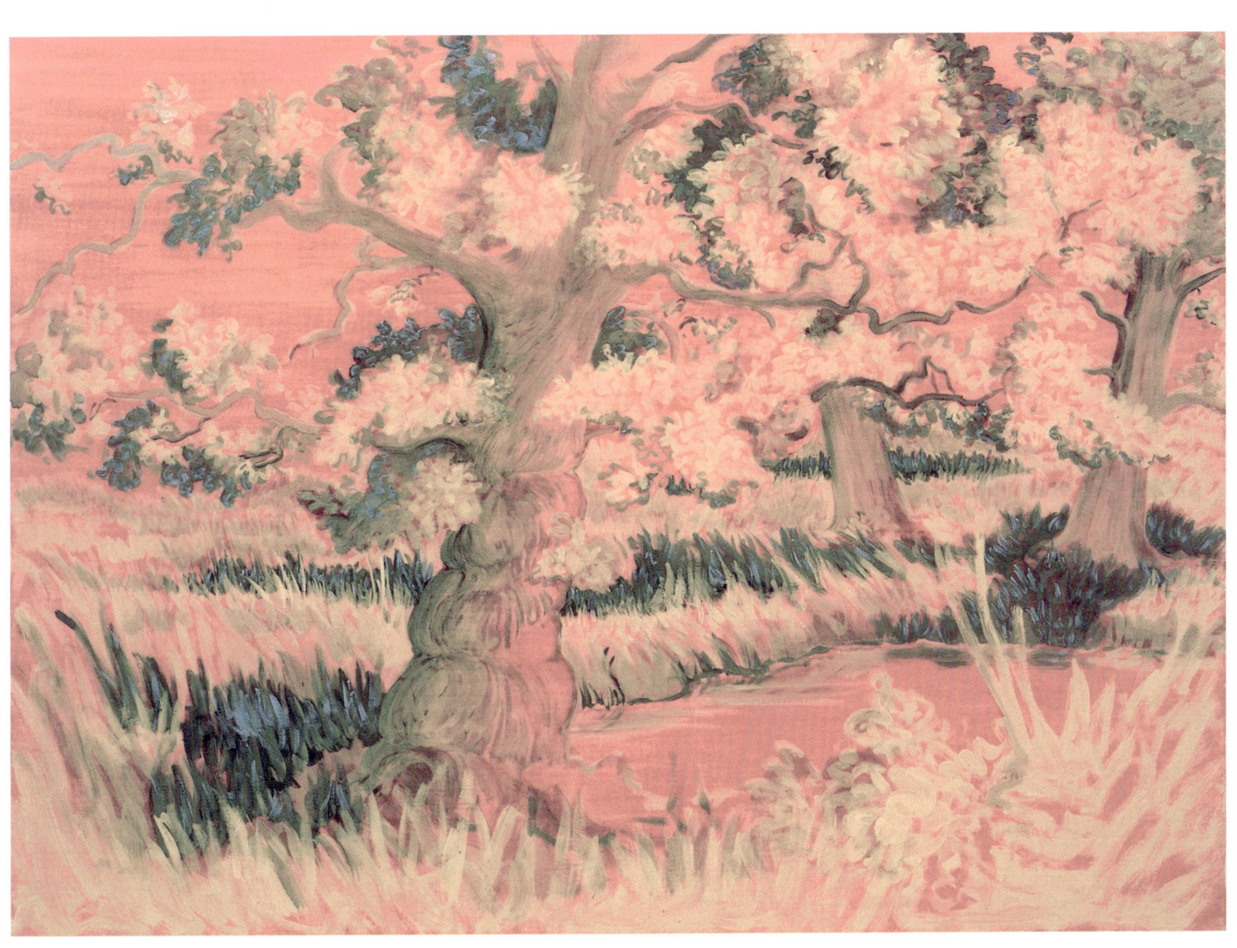

10   **The Steps of Man**  2007
fluorescent lemon yellow, Cadmium lemon yellow, Cobalt turquoise egg
tempera; Prussian blue, French gold ochre, lead antimonate, raw Siena,
red lead, bone black, lead white in oils; birch leaf lake in pine resin on board
102 x 122 cm

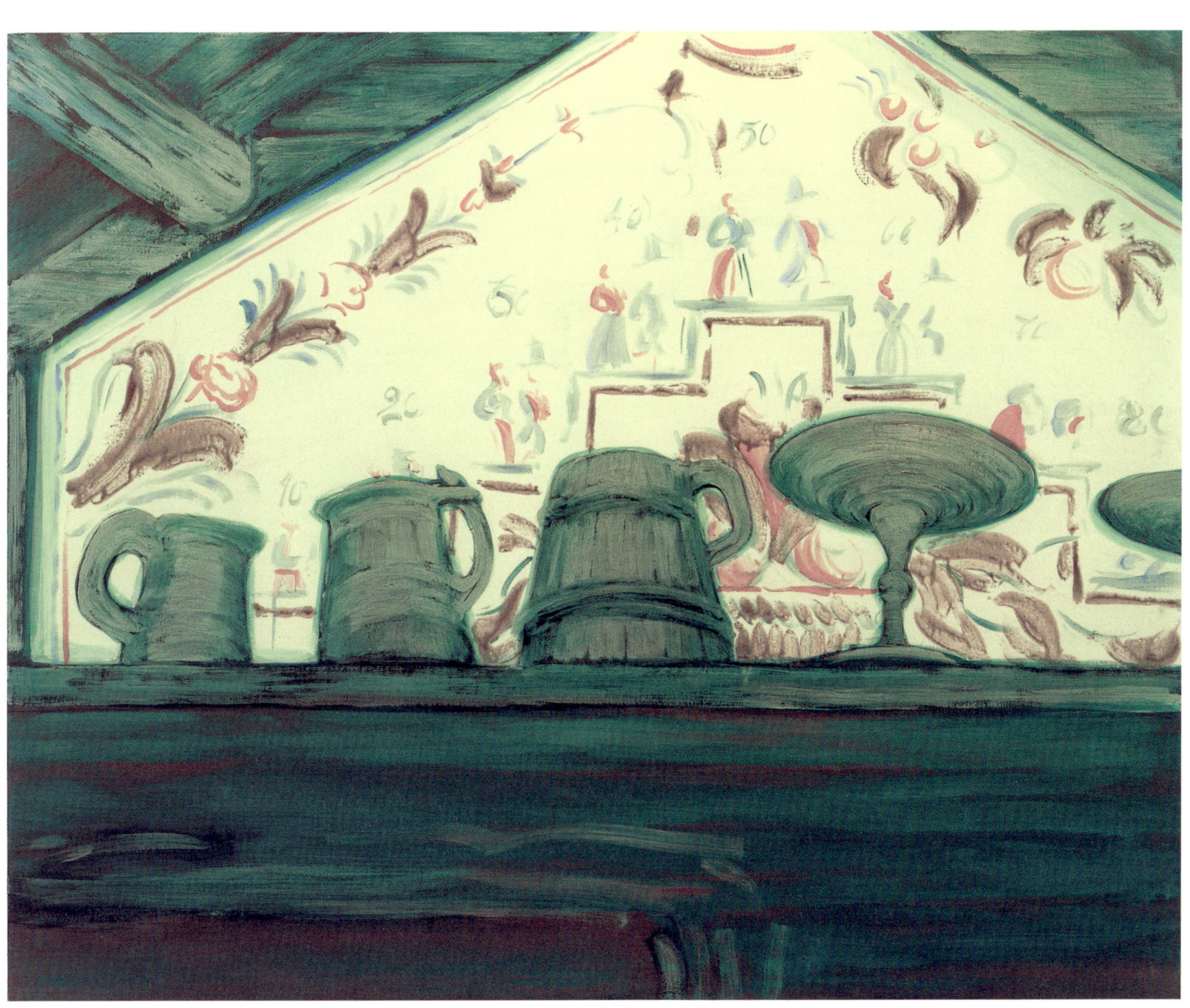

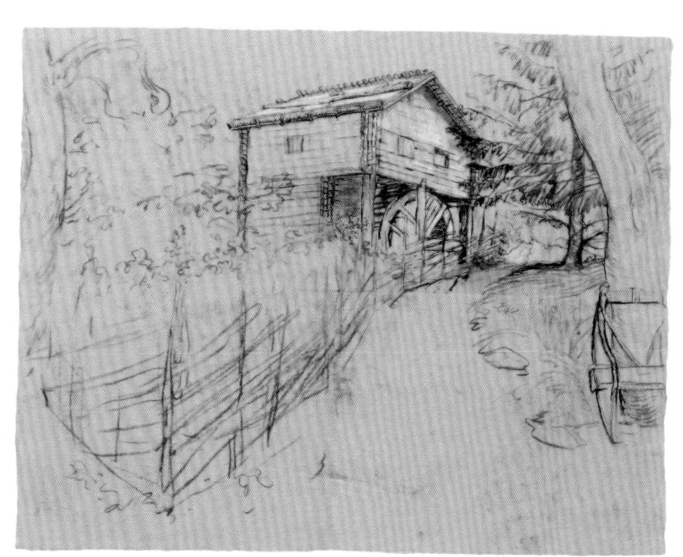

11   **The Linen Mill**  2007
fluorescent flame red egg tempera; lead white, Bohemian green earth,
Viridian, Cobalt turquoise, Cochineal, Chrome yellow in oils on board
74 x 91 cm

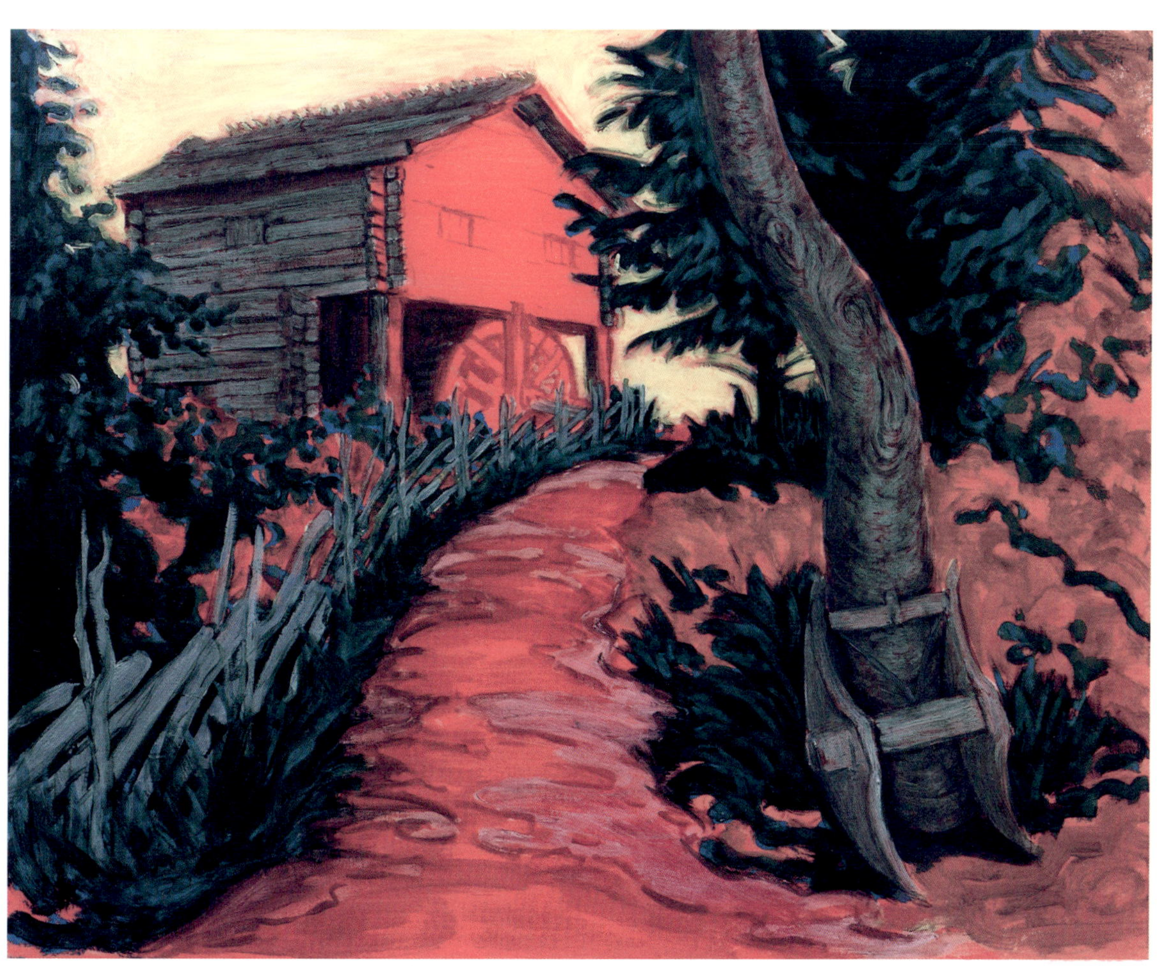

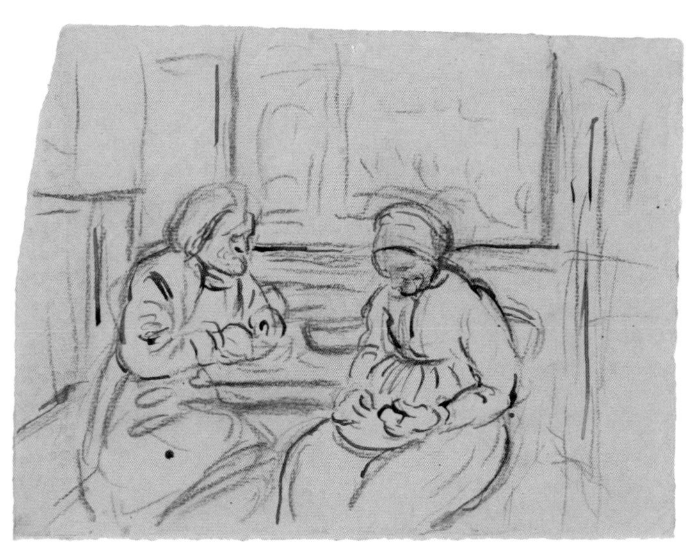

**12**  **The Last Peasant-Painters Peeling Potatoes (Old Woman Mill)**  2007
fluorescent orange egg tempera; lead white, Prussian blue, Chrome yellow
light, lead antimonate, Bohemian green earth, Spanish glazing ochre; iron
oxide in soured milk; birch leaf lake in pine resin on board
122 x 142 cm

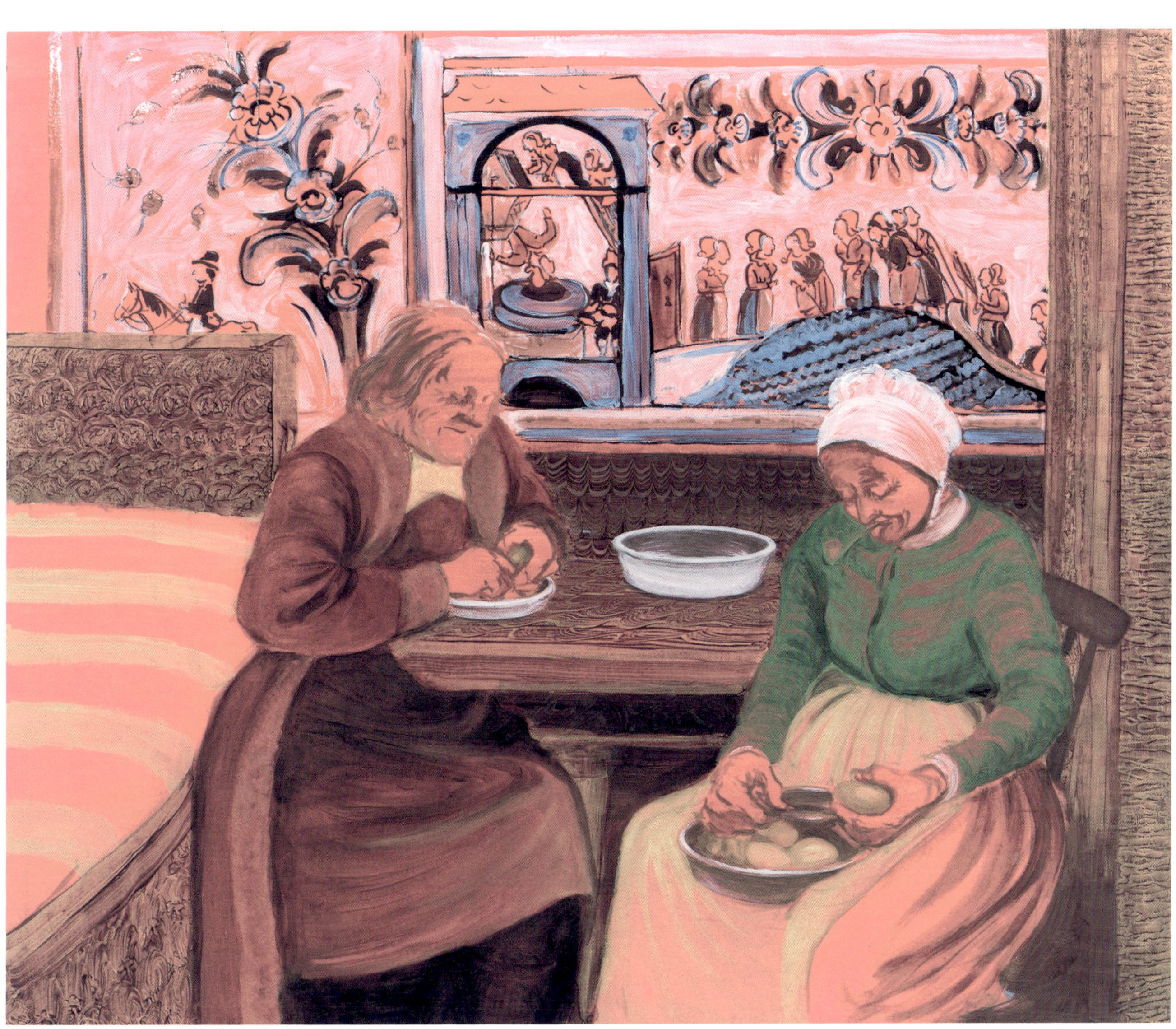

13  **The Älvros Farmstead**  2007
Cobalt turquoise, zinc white, fluorescent lemon yellow egg tempera;
Prussian blue, Cadmium red vermillioned, Chrome yellow light, lead
antimonate in oils; fluorescent lemon yellow in soured milk on board
107 x 122 cm

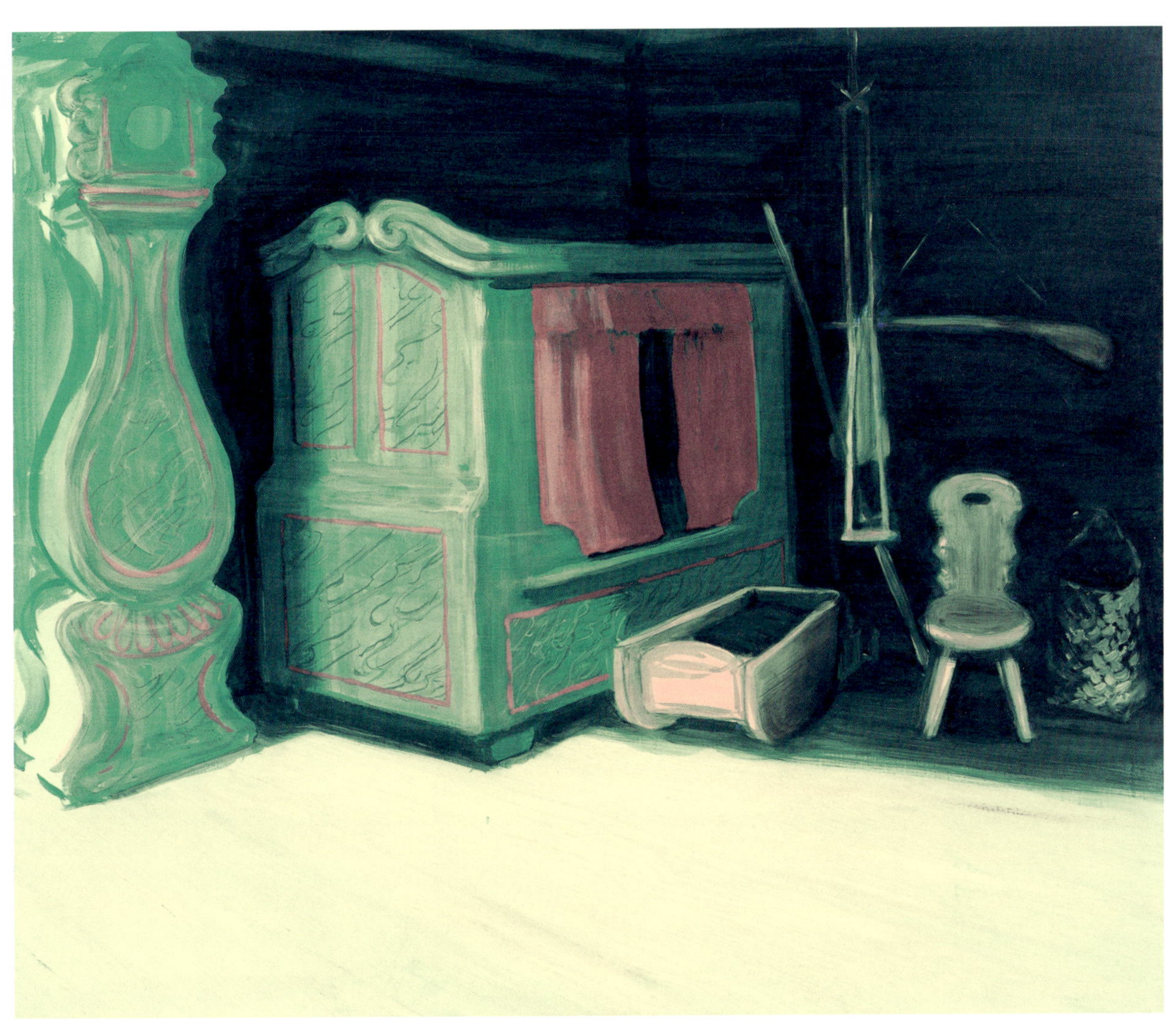

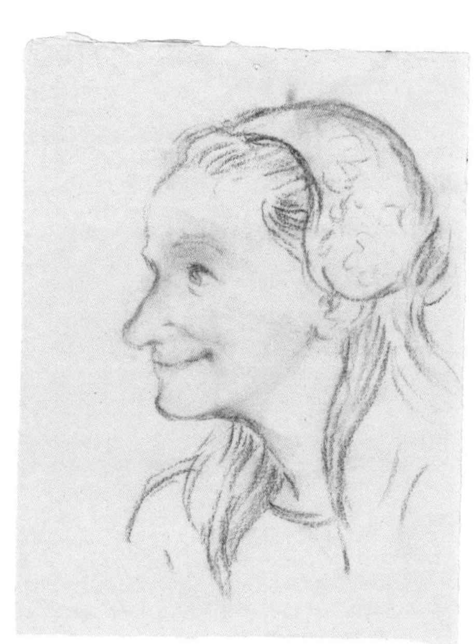

**14**  **Girl with a Distaff (Betrothal)**  2007
fluorescent brick red egg tempera; red lead, lead white, Spanish
glazing ochre, French ultramarine, Cobalt turquoise, lead antimonate
in oils; fluorescent brick red in soured milk on board
75 x 61 cm

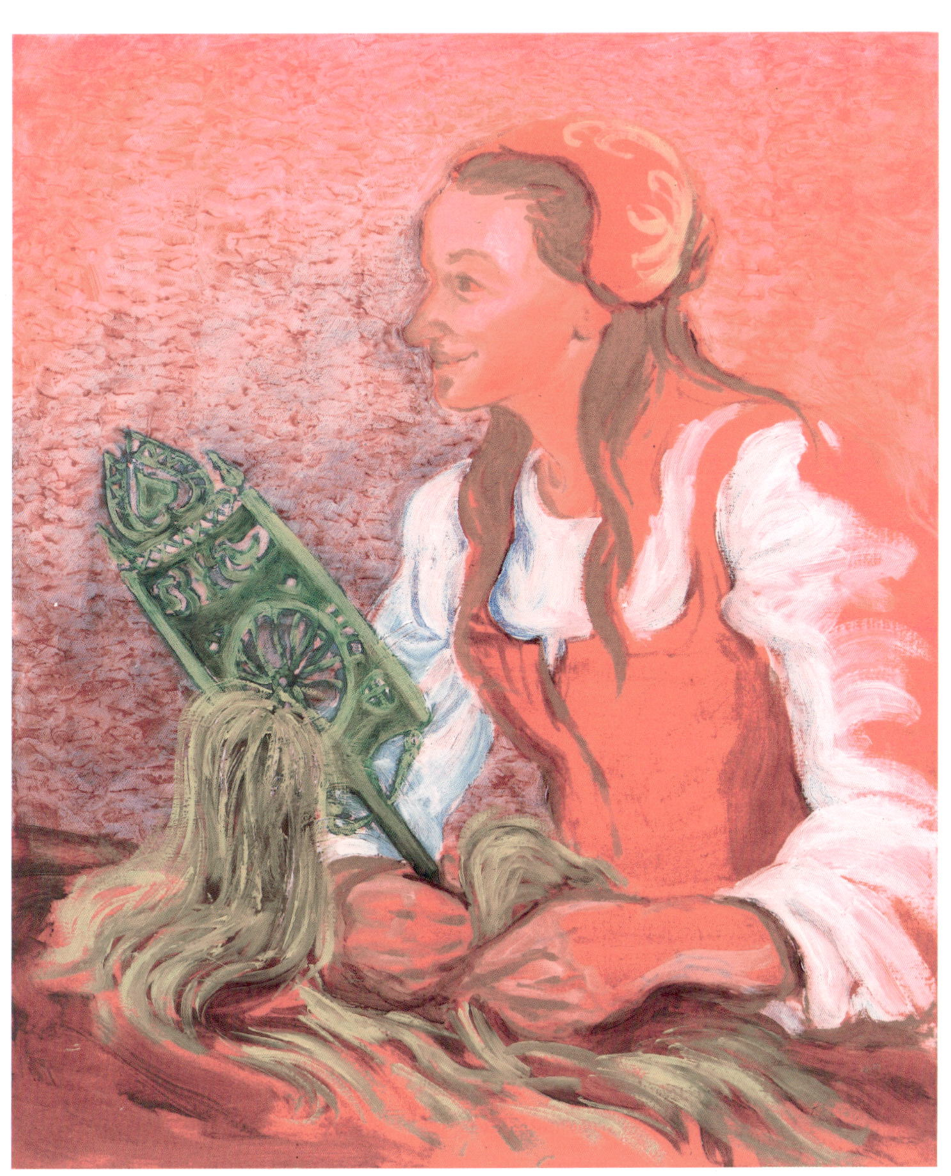

15  **The Young Folk Sleep with the Animals in Summer**  2007
fluorescent yellow orange, raw Siena, Chrome yellow, lead
antimonate, Viridian, lead white, French ultramarine in
oils on board
74 x 91 cm

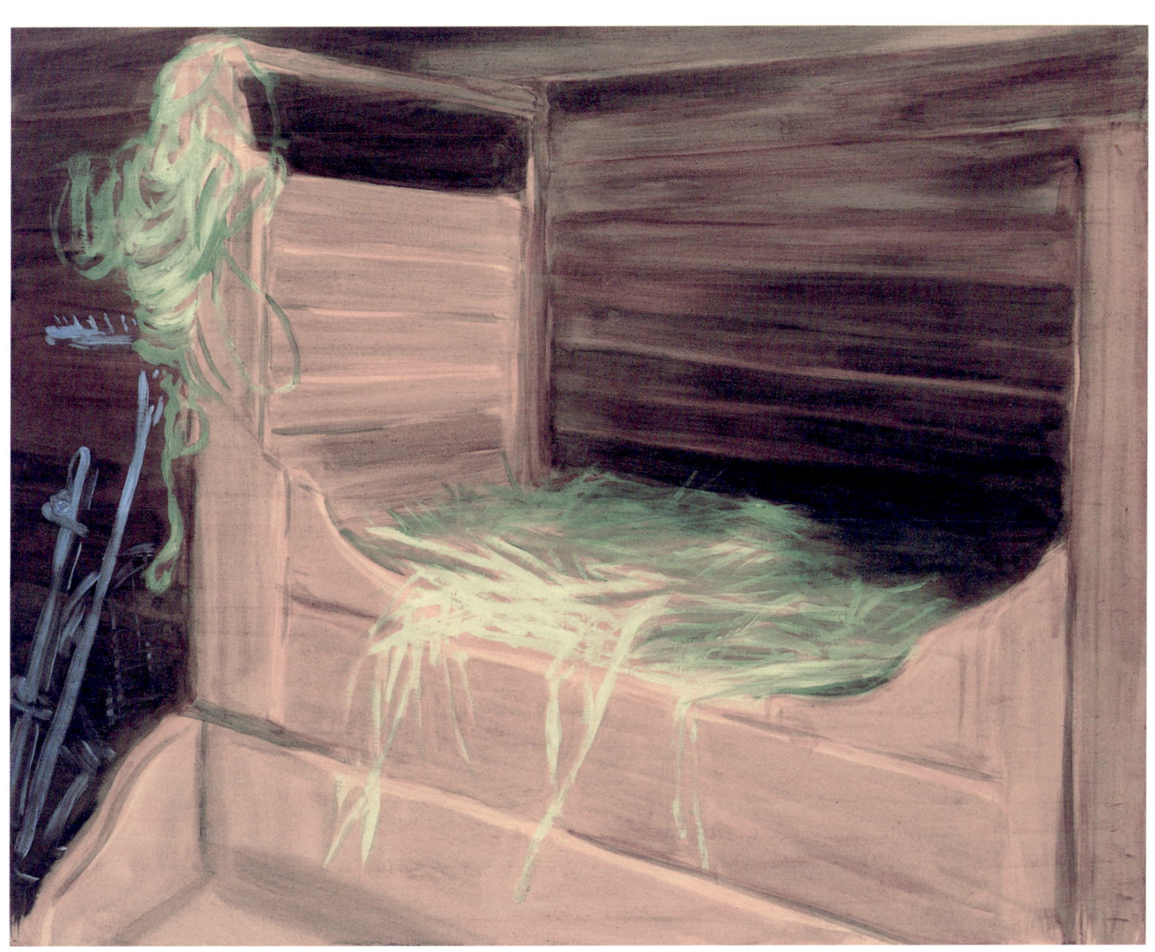

16  **Wedding Feast**  2007
fluorescent yellow orange, Cochineal egg tempera; lead white,
bone black, red lead, lead white, Chrome yellow light, lead antimonate,
Chrome green, Bohemian green earth, Viridian in oils on board
122 x 142 cm

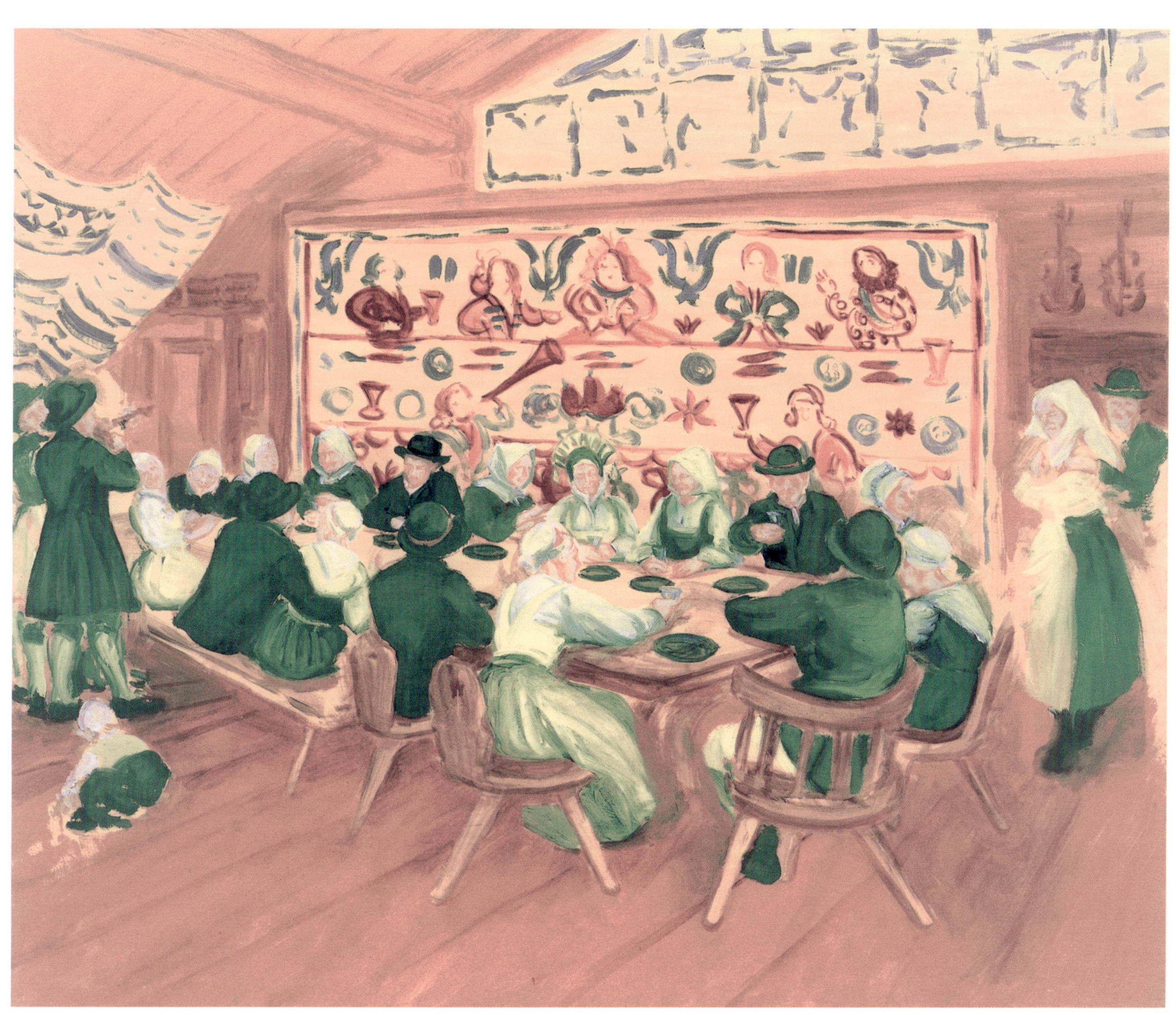

17   **The Oktorp Farmstead**  2007
fluorescent orange egg tempera; Spanish glazing ochre,
Chrome yellow, lead antimonate, Viridian, red lead in oils on board
75 x 61 cm

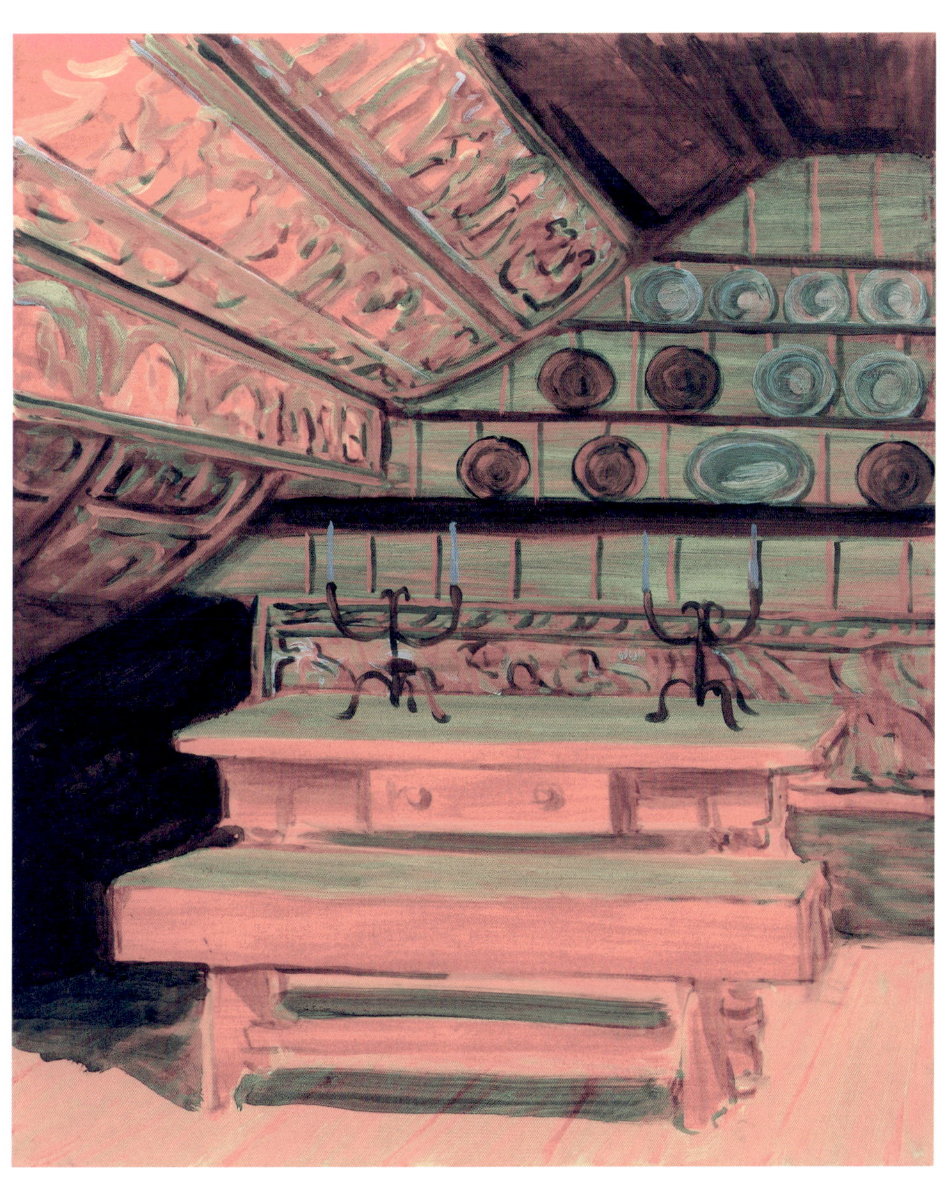

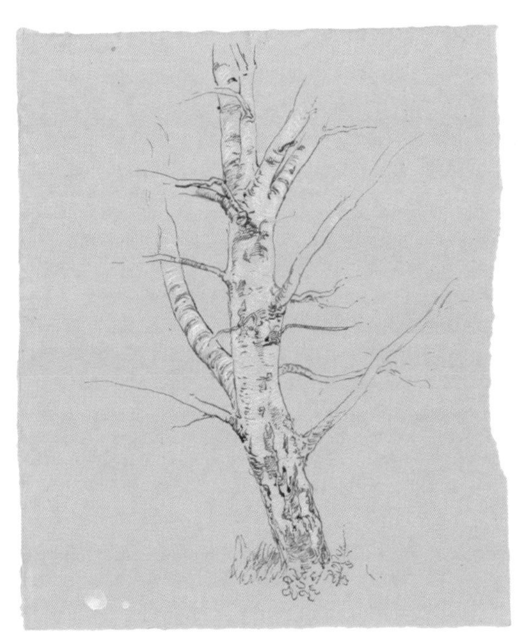

18  **The Birches**  2007
Cobalt turquoise, zinc white, fluorescent lemon yellow egg tempera;
Spanish glazing ochre, lead white, Viridian in oils on board
122 x 91 cm

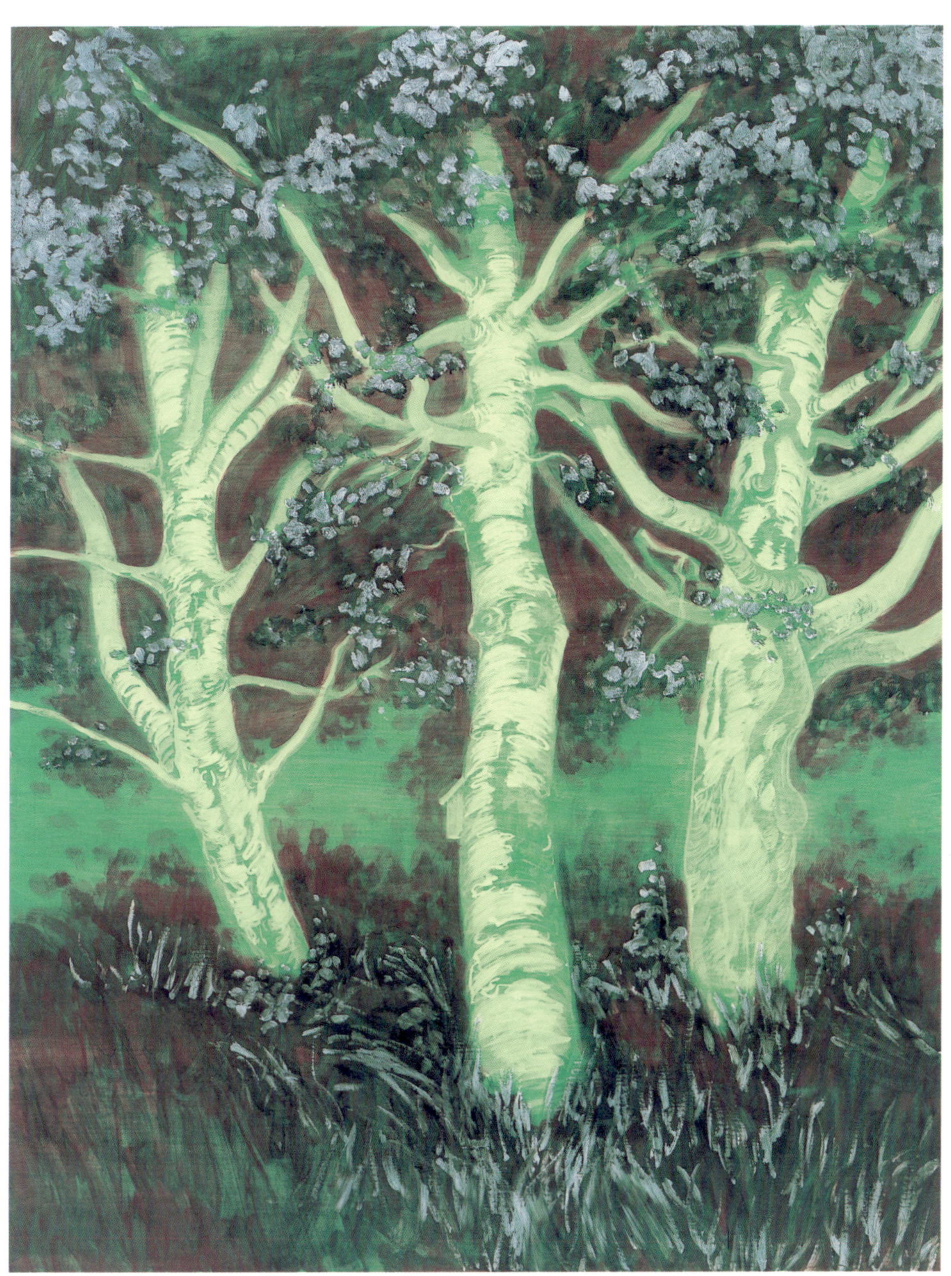

19  **Woven Logs**  2007
fluorescent yellow orange egg tempera; Cochineal, madder,
lead white, French ultramarine in oils on board
75 x 61 cm

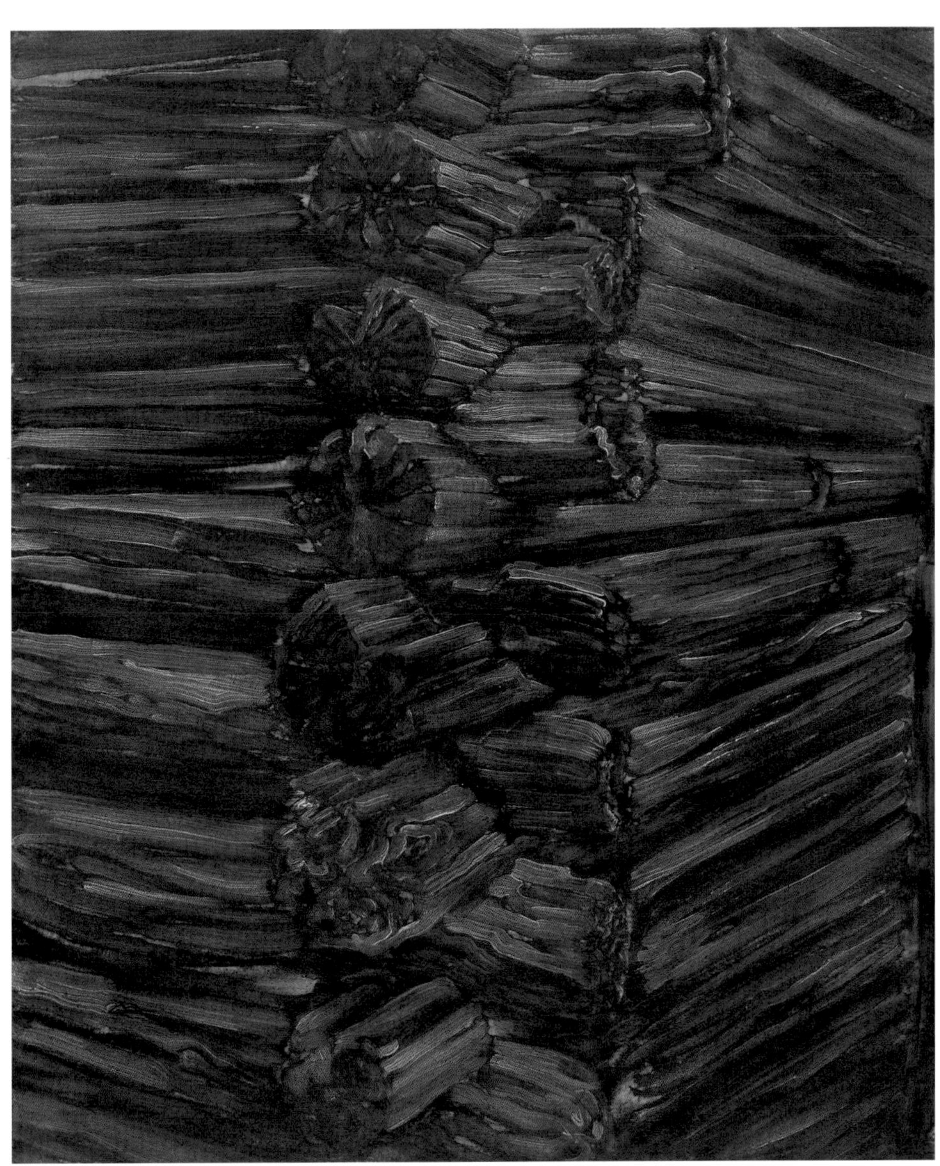

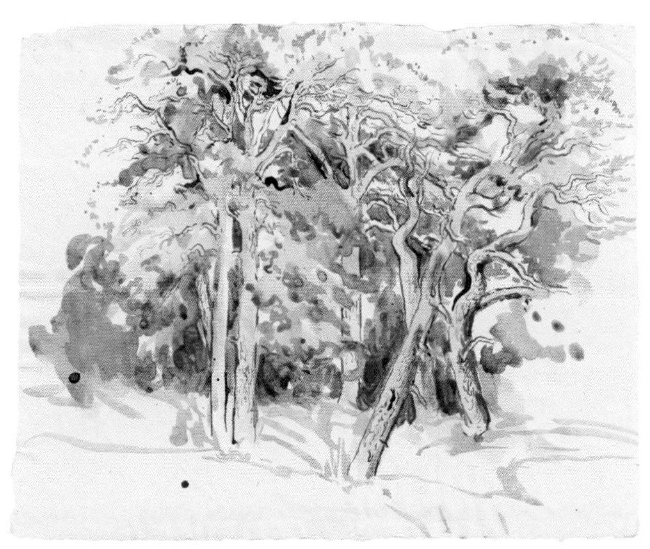

20   **The Pines**  2007
Cobalt blue, zinc white, fluorescent yellow orange egg tempera;
Chrome yellow, Bohemian green earth, Cochineal in oils on board
53 x 60 cm

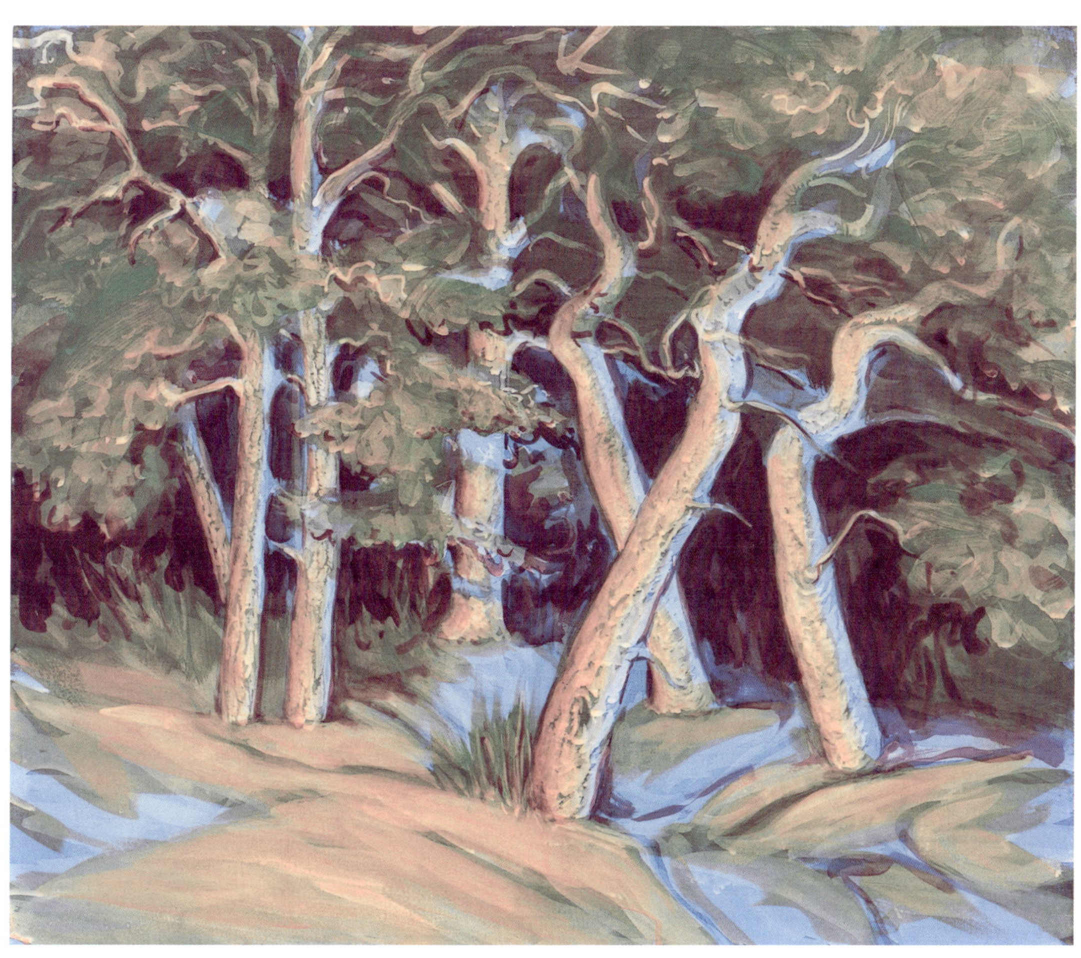

21  **Europa**  2007
fluorescent brick red egg tempera; Chrome yellow light,
lead antimonate, lead white, red lead, Viridian, Chrome
green, Cobalt turquoise in oils on board
61 x 75 cm

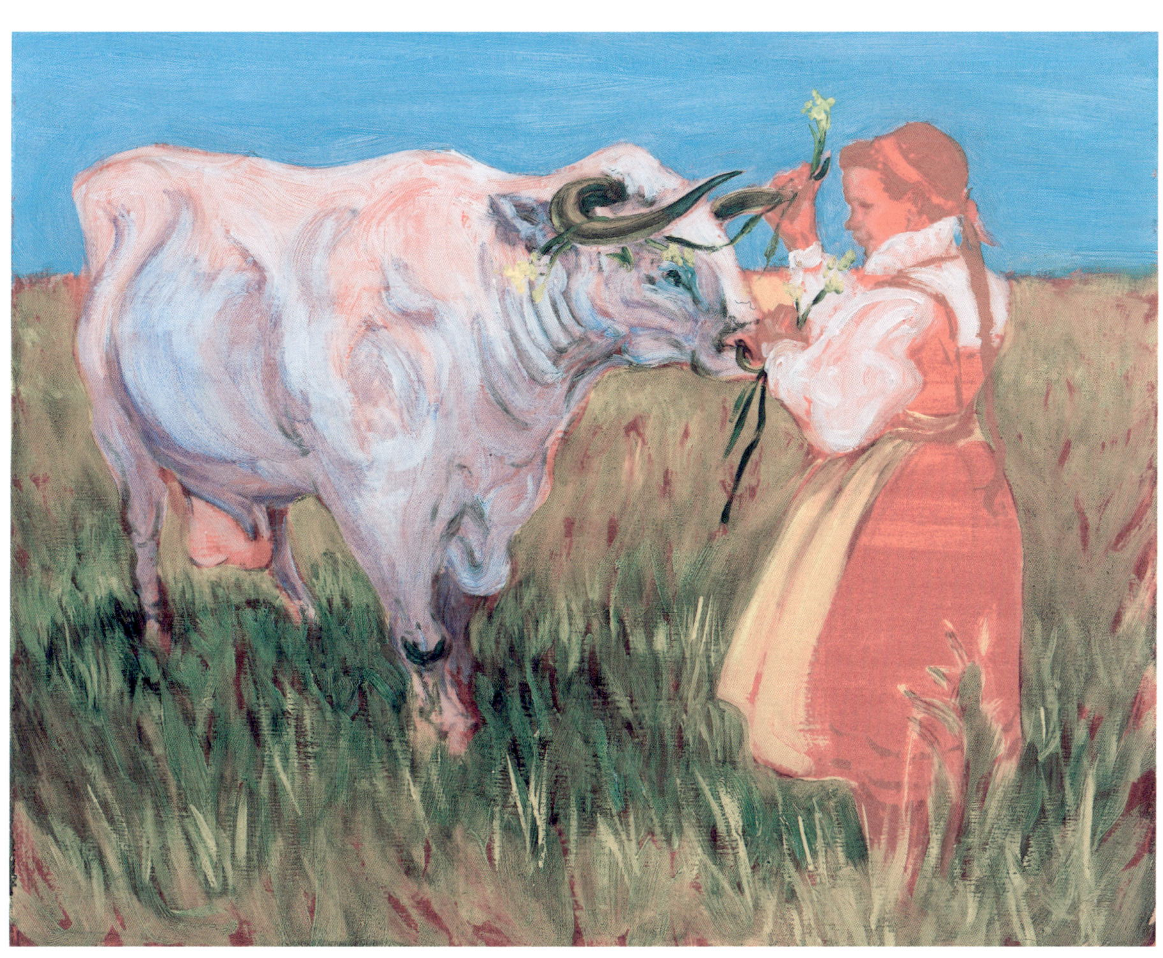

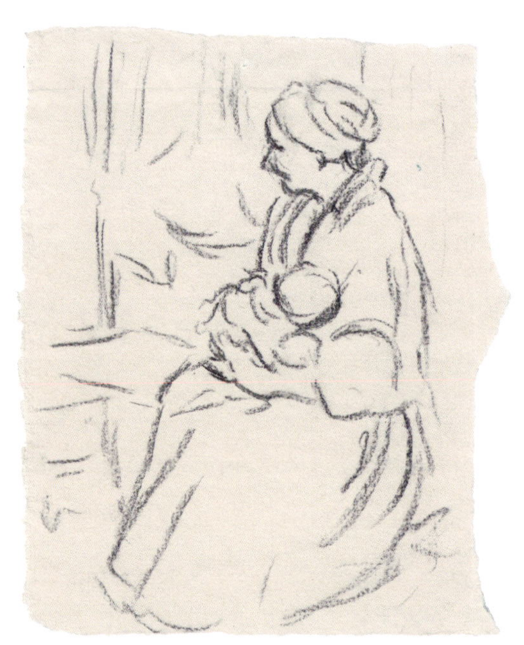

22  **Mother and Child**  2007
fluorescent brick red egg tempera; Cobalt turquoise, lead antimonate,
red lead, lead white, Prussian blue in oils; iron oxide in soured milk on board
91 x 74 cm

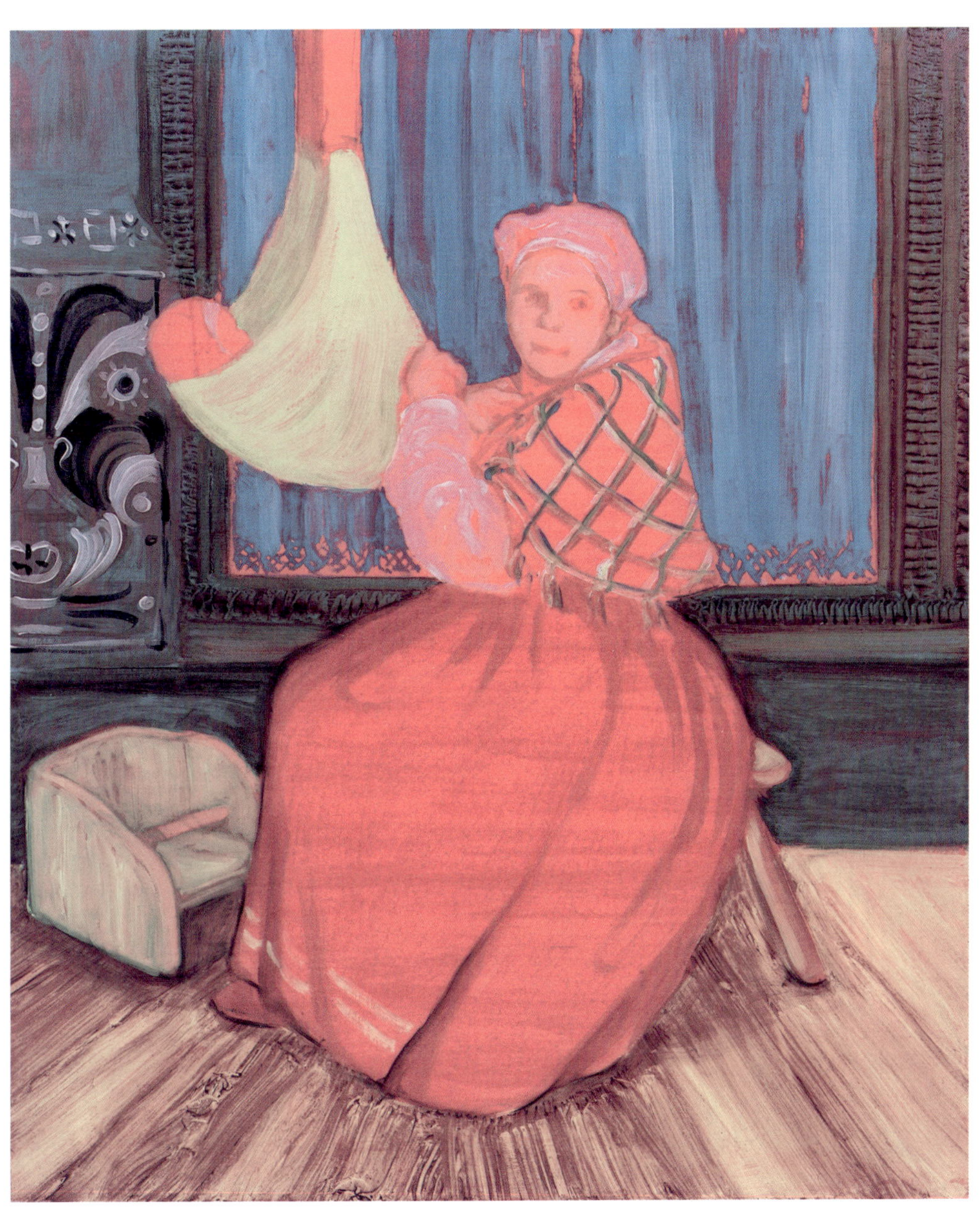

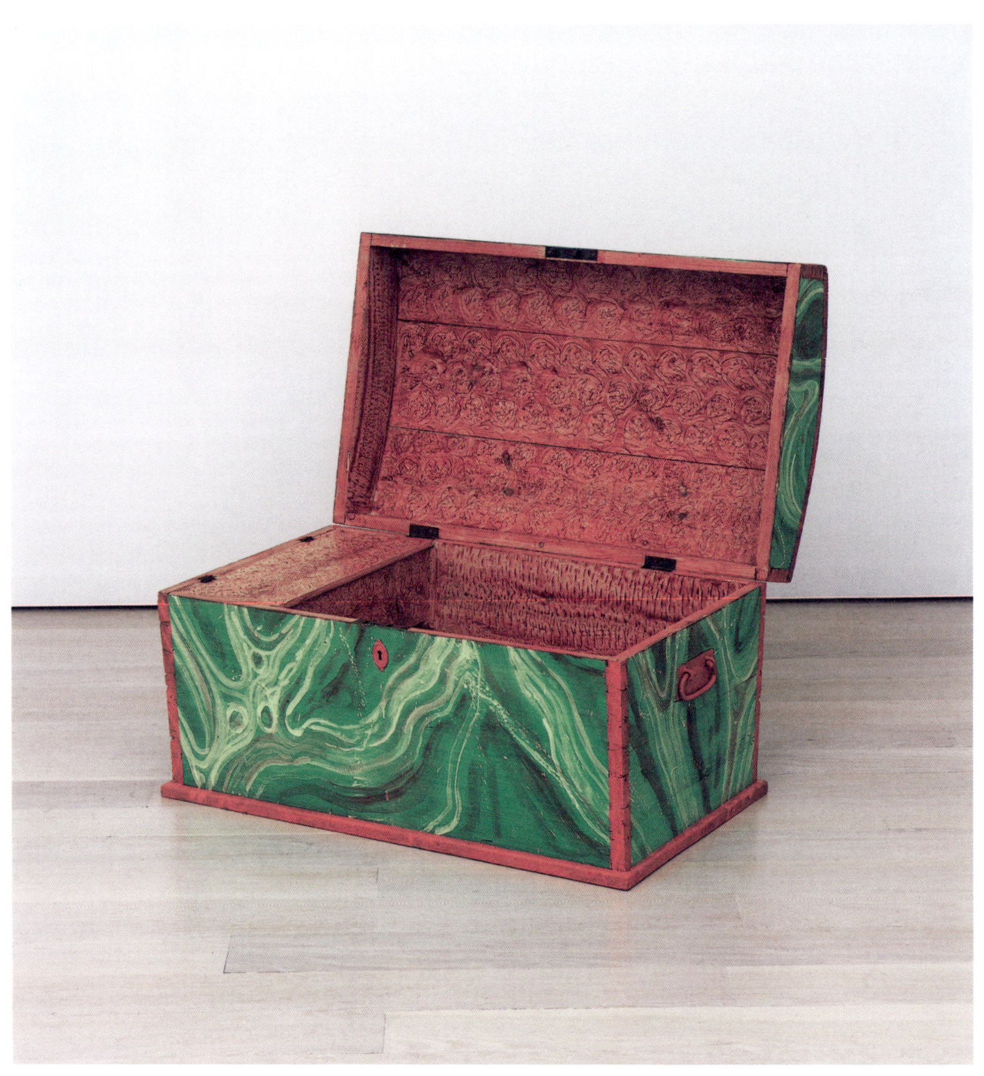

23  **Bride's Chest**  2007
Cobalt turquoise, zinc white, fluorescent lemon yellow in egg-oil emulsion; iron oxide, red lead, lead antimonate in oils; iron oxide in soured milk on 19th century bride's chest
41 x 75 x 47 cm

## Biography

Born 19 November 1978
2000-2002     MA in Painting, Royal College of Art, London
1997-2000     BFA, Ruskin School of Drawing and Fine Art, Oxford
Lives and works in London


## Selected Solo Exhibitions

2007        *1857 - Paintings*, Annely Juda Fine Art, London
2006        *Past-times and Re-creation*, Transition, London
            *Self-sufficient*, Contemporary Arts Projects, London
2004        *la Pittura Sale sugli Alberi*, 42contemporaneo, Modena, Italy


## Selected Group Exhibitions

2007        *Annely Juda - A Celebration*, Annely Juda Fine Art, London
            *Artificial Glory*, Standpoint Gallery, London
            *Cunning Chapters*, The British Library, London
2006        *The Spiral of Time*, APT, London; touring to OHOA, Reading
            *Responding to Rome*, Estorick Collection, London
2005        *The Jerwood Drawing Prize 2005*, Jerwood Space, London (touring)
            *Hand in Hand we walk alone*, Clapham Art Gallery, London
            *Pocket-Scopic*, Sartorial Contemporary Art, London
2004        *If you go down to the woods today...*, Rockwell Gallery, London
            *Spazi Aperti*, Romanian Academy, Rome, Italy
            *Extra-Natura: Konst! Scopriamo la Svezia*, 42contemporaneo, Modena, Italy
            *Compass*, Sala 1, Rome, Italy
2003        *Bloomberg New Contemporaries 2003*, Manchester and London
            *Vaguely Romantic*, Rosie Wilde, London
            *Rockwell*, Rockwell Gallery London


## Awards

2003-04     Sainsbury Scholarship in Painting and Sculpture at the British
            School at Rome


## Selected Bibliography

Garageland, Paradox, Practice and Piss Pigment, Alex Michon, Issue 3, 2007
Dazed and Confused, Atmosphere, Nick Hackworth and Peter Stitson, July 2005, p.85
Arte Critica, Holmwood/Lundgren/Olsson, Vania Granata, April-June 2004, p.71
Flash Art, Compass, Patrizia Ferri, April-May 2004, p.156
Arte Critica, L'ona della YBA a Roma, Francesca De Nicolo, April-June 2004, p.52
Compass: review, Edith Schloss, Wanted in Rome, 18 February 2004, p.12
la Pittura Sale sugli Alberi, Catalogue, 2004
Konst! Scopriamo La Svezia, Catalogue, 2004
Bloomberg New Contemporaries 2003, Catalogue, 2003

ISBN 1-904621-21-X

Photographs of the works: Ian Parker

Essay: Paul Bonaventura

Catalogue © Annely Juda Fine Art/Sigrid Holmwood 2008

Printed by BAS Printers, England